# How Mommy Got Her Groove Back
by Rebecca Undem

Kittleson Creek Press
10719 390th St. SE
Fertile, MN 56540

Printed in U.S.A.

rebeccaundem.com

Library of Congress Number: 2016943162

ISBN 978-0-9881856-2-3

# Dedication

This book is dedicated to my children: Andrew, Carter, and Brynlee. May you always have the courage to make your own paths. Wander, my loves.

# Acknowledgements

I owe the biggest thank-you to the individuals specifically named within this book. Without the love and encouragement of my personal support system and without the wisdom, guidance, and advice of my professional support system, this book wouldn't exist. I am eternally grateful.

## The Last Grandparent

I pull next to the curb outside the Oakes Good Samaritan Center and stop behind my parents' burnt orange Dodge Ram truck. As I shift into park, my phone dings with the notification of a new message. I decide to quickly respond to the email before heading in to meet my mom.

Just as I finish typing the last of the email, my phone rings. "Hey, Mom."

"Are you almost here?" she asks.

"I just pulled up. Be right in."

She quietly replies, "Okay."

With that one word, I *know.* It is not okay. He is gone.

Snatching up my purse, I stride to the north side of the building and tug open the heavy metal door to the nursing home and head straight to the room three doors down on the left. As I approach the threshold, Mom meets me.

"He's … gone." Her voice is thick. Choked. She rushes forward to throw her arms around my neck. We fold into each other as the initial sobs of sorrow shake us in unison.

"I'm so sorry I wasn't here," I say through my tears. "I was just outside sending a stupid email that could have waited for later."

"It's all right. I almost didn't get here myself. When I came in, his breathing was so ragged that I knew it was time. I was here holding his hand when he took his last breath. I'm just so thankful he wasn't alone."

I walk farther into the room and turn to see Grandpa Seefeldt. Still and at peace. A stark contrast to yesterday when he struggled with agitation and discomfort.

"Oh, Grandpa!" I kneel next to his bed and touch his hand, his chest. Although now lifeless, his body is still warm.

Mom and I hold each other for a few more minutes before I leave the room to make the necessary calls. I need to break the news to Dad, my husband, my brother, and our minister.

As we wait for family to arrive, the nursing home staff congregates in Grandpa's room to hold a bedside service. We read Scripture aloud together and listen as the staff share thoughts about Grandpa.

"He was the happiest guy you ever did meet."

"He was never in a bad mood."

"He was one of the easiest residents to care for."

After a comforting prayer, we hug staff members who had become friends. Friends that had loved and served Grandpa for the five years following Grandma Seefeldt's unexpected death, when the family made the difficult choice to move him here.

On the television stand, Mom picks up a picture of her parents and holds it to her chest. "Well, they're together now."

We share a bittersweet chuckle at the idea of Grandma Seefeldt standing there with her slightly gap-toothed smile, her arms wide open, declaring, "Welcome home, Howie, welcome home."

In spite of my sadness at losing my last grandparent, I feel a deep sense of gratitude. I'm grateful for this moment. This sacred, precious moment. I get to be here. I get to be the first person to hug Mom. To love her through the pain. I'm her "person."

Later that morning, Mom's siblings arrive. After Aunt Karen and Uncle Dan have their time alone with Grandpa, they enter the nursing home's lounge where the rest of us wait.

After a tearful greeting, I ask, "What now? Do you need to go straight to the funeral home?"

They all shrug, obviously numb and unfocused at this recent turn of events.

I take charge and offer, "Well, you all need to eat. Why don't you come over to our place and we'll fix you lunch. Then you can figure out what to do from there."

My husband Jeremiah and I drive to the grocery store to get some things to pull together a fast meal.

Back at our house, they shuffle in and find seats. We eat in a silence pierced only by bits of meaningless conversation. As I clean the kitchen and start prepping soup for our dinner that night, they open a discussion about the funeral service. Mom takes on the role she excels at: management.

Mom is a handler, a fixer. When there are things to be done, she does them. When there are problems to be solved, she solves them. When there are decisions to be made, she makes them. Being the oldest at the table, she handles the task of leading the family through the decisions of planning the service.

Pastor had given her a helpful list of suggestions for readings and hymns and Mom asks Uncle Dan to read them aloud to the family. As he reads the passages, emotion overwhelms him. "I'm sorry, I really struggle reading these verses out loud." Jeremiah opens his Bible and reads the remaining text. The family quickly selects three verses.

"When it comes to the music," Mom says, "Dad only requested one hymn for his funeral—'Be Still My Soul.' Is everyone okay with that? Good. And I'd really love to have Tom and Becky sing 'When Peace Like a River,' the same song we had at Mom's funeral."

Incredulous, I turn from the kitchen counter. "Really, Mom? You want me to sing *that song* with Dad? Since Grandma's funeral, I haven't been able to even hear it without crying."

I look at Dad but he just shrugs. I know he'll do whatever she wants him to do.

My mom gazes at me and, without a hint of sarcasm or challenge, asks, "Don't you want to make your mother happy, Becky?"

With a knowing look, I face her square on. "Of course I do, Mom. I really do."

It is settled. I will sing.

As they continue with their planning, I chop vegetables and reflect on how much of my life has been about pleasing other people. *I've suffered from the "disease to please" for much of my life,* I think. But this time, even though she directly challenged me to please her, I didn't feel handled. I didn't feel managed. I said yes because I *wanted* to.

Pleasing Mom pleases me.

Later that night as my fragrant homemade soup perfumes the kitchen, the weight of Grandpa's death still hangs like a thick blanket of humidity. Although it's swept aside by spurts of laughter when my three young children delight us, my eyes continue to mist over as I recognize fully that family is everything to me.

Oh, I've casually said, "Family is everything," with the hollow meaning of any other flippant cliché you'd see cross-stitched on a pillow at your nana's house.

This is different. I am *living* it.

For the first time since returning to Oakes, I can see the immeasurable value of being right here. It was a realization that evokes all five of my senses.

I see it in the sad, yet still smiling faces of my loved ones.

I smell it and taste it through our shared meal. Our family has always been big into food. It's what we do. We do food.

I feel and hear it through my oldest son, Andrew, when he comments how sad he is for Grandma Jeanie; my unknowing and innocent daughter, Brynlee, smacking my face, causing me to chide, "Gentle, Brynlee, be gentle;" the goodbye hugs from Karen's husband, Halder, when he and Uncle Dan leave to go tell the absent sibling Gary, who lives in a nursing home sixty miles away, his father has died; and the tugs at my heart when Carter dissolves everyone's tears with the typical, rowdy antics of a four-year-old boy.

I am here, with my family. My new family and my old family, together, in one place. It's my past crashing into my present. And in this sacred union, I see my future. It suddenly feels as if the long road I took to get to this exact place was exactly as it needed to be.

The road is my story. And my story begins with my parents, before I was born.

# Smooth Talker

Despite the hot, sticky July night, Jeanie Seefeldt tried everything she could to stay focused on the task at hand.

As people responded to her standard issue greeting, "Welcome to Dairy Queen, how may I help you?" by ordering their burgers and shakes, as she wiped counters and counted back change, she couldn't quell the excitement of where she'd be in just a few short weeks.

A freshly minted graduate of the class of 1972, she couldn't wait to leave the small town of Oakes, North Dakota, to begin her new life in Minneapolis, Minnesota, where she would attend a two-year program to become a medical assistant. She'd always been mature for her age. She'd had little choice in the matter.

In the summer of 1961, then six-year-old Jeanie was playing with her little sister Karen in the yard on their Wisconsin farm while their brother Gary played at the Raster farm, just over the field and across the gravel road. Their mother Dorothy worked in the garden.

Suddenly, Burt Raster came running across the field screaming. All three looked up. Even though they couldn't make out his words, they knew something was terribly wrong. Dorothy raced across the field, leaving Jeanie and Karen behind.

*What should I do?* Jeanie wondered. *Should I follow Mom?*

At that moment, Rita, who lived just past the Raster farm, drove into the yard on a tractor. Seeing the girls standing alone, she told them to climb aboard.

When they arrived at her farm, Rita immediately hopped off the tractor and ran to see what was happening next door.

"Stay here," Jeanie ordered Karen, and she jumped off to follow Rita.

Jeanie found her mom, Rita, and the Rasters standing under a tall oak tree over Gary, sprawled—unmoving—on the ground. A dark purple bruise started appearing along the side of his face. Certain he was dead, Jeanie started to bawl.

Dorothy looked over her shoulder. "Get her out of here!"

As Rita whisked her away, Jeanie stole a last glance at her best friend, this brother only a mere year older who was her favorite playmate.

Back at Rita's, Karen was inconsolable, wanting her mom. Young Jeanie stepped up and did her best to comfort her three-year-old sister until Grandma Western arrived to take them home.

Gary was not dead. But, because of a daredevil fall from the tallest tree in the Raster's yard, he had suffered an extensive traumatic brain injury (TBI). He spent several weeks in the hospital's Intensive Care Unit (ICU) before transferring to the Rehabilitative Unit where he would learn to talk, walk, and eat again. Vibrant, energetic Gary was no more.

Dorothy spent every day at the hospital with her young son, returning home each night. During this difficult time, Grandma Western and Grandma Seefeldt came to care for the children.

One evening when her mom got home, Jeanie could see she was spent—physically, emotionally, and mentally exhausted. Her mom laid her head on Grandma Western's shoulder and crumpled into her, the weight of the situation crushing her spirit.

Jeanie had never seen her mother sob like that before. *Oh, my poor mom. My poor dad. My poor family,* she thought

As with any traumatic event, it took time to establish a new normal. Initially, every struggle her parents had to assimilate the new Gary into his old life served as a painful reminder of the future they'd lost. The future Gary had lost. Jeanie felt compassion for her family and a sense of responsibility far beyond her tender years.

When Dan was born just four years later, she believed he was "her" special baby, given to their family exclusively for her to love and tend. She became the ultimate nurturer, making her a hot commodity for local parents who needed a babysitter.

When Jeanie was twelve, the family moved to Oakes so that her dad could work at the Western Cheese Factory owned by her Uncle Norman. Jeanie continued babysitting in her new community and got a job at the Dairy Queen a couple of years later.

Although she loved being a nurturer and hoped to have a family of her own one day, Jeanie was ready for an adventure. An adventure all her own.

Daydreaming about the hustle and bustle of the city, she recalled a conversation she'd had earlier that week when she and her friend Nancy cruised Main.

"Jeanie, I know an older guy who wants to date you," Nancy revealed, smiling like the Cheshire cat.

"Uh, I don't really think I'm interested," she'd coolly replied.

"Well, I think you'll be interested once you know who it is." Nancy paused for effect. "It's Tom Rodine!"

"You're shitting me!" Jeanie said. "Why on earth would Tom Rodine be interested in me? He's so much older—and he's so cool. Seriously?"

"See, I told you you'd be interested!" Nancy crossed her arms in satisfaction. "He told me he wants to ask you out. Just thought you should know."

Now, Jeanie considered what she really knew about Tom Rodine. Each time he showed up at the Dairy Queen, he was friendly and chatty with everyone who worked there, but the two of them had never had a real conversation. She had seen his band, the Dynamic Dischords, perform once, but there was no way he even noticed her there. *I'm just one girl in a crowd of girls that night.* She sighed.

As she walked to her car after closing that night, Tom approached her in the parking lot. Without a word, he offered his right arm to her, and she accepted!

As famous as Tom Rodine was for being a smooth talker, my dad snagged his first date with my mom without saying a single word to her.

## Silent Surrender

My mom was a looker.

Of course, everybody believes her mother has a special brand of beauty. But mine was gorgeous in an obvious-to-everyone-with-eyes kind of way. Around five-foot-eight, with legs that went on for miles and a thin wiry frame, she parted her long, shiny hair down the middle *a la* 1970s. Like many women who never fully embrace their beauty, she saw herself as awkward, gangly, and knock-kneed. But, with her wide, vivacious smile, Jeanie Seefeldt looked like a supermodel.

My dad's been known to say that he's not sure what appealed to him more when he first met Mom: her mile-high legs in a short work skirt or her scent of hamburger-and-fries. What a charmer. Although he was a smooth talker and appeared confident and self-assured, he reminisces about how he felt the first time Jeanie Seefeldt put her hand through his bent arm. He felt like he'd won the lottery.

A couple of weeks into their new relationship, Jeanie's parents (Howard and Dorothy) sat her down in the kitchen.

"We can't let you go off to college without getting this off our minds," Dorothy began.

"Please know, Jean, we think Tom is a great guy," Howard started. "But …"

Jeanie sensed where this conversation was going.

"… we both have concerns about his age. He's so much older than you."

*Is eight years really that much older?* Jeanie wondered. *I mean, I get it. But really, I've always been mature and the guys I dated through high school just seemed so … young. I like that he's older and has a plan for his life. Plus, he has a really nice car. I feel safe with him. Secure with him. Not that I'd ever say this out loud to Mom and Dad.*

"We want to make sure that nothing gets in the way of your plans to attend school and make something of yourself. We can see that you really care for him, and we're concerned that you need to slow this down or the relationship might cloud your thinking." Her mom raised her brows, waiting for Jeanie to respond.

"I understand what you're saying, but I'm not sure how I can slow this down."

Exchanging a worried look, her parents answered almost in unison. "We just want you to know how we feel."

Jeanie nodded. *But I'm not sure what I'm supposed to do about it, exactly.*

As she packed for college, she had mixed feelings, uncertain how her relationship with Tom would continue with her living nearly five hours away. Tom was a fourth-generation farmer and had never left Oakes for formal schooling. His plan was to continue farming. This was certainly a worrisome factor as she considered her future, but she really did want to go off to school.

As her parents drove her to Minneapolis, Jeanie tingled with anticipation—*almost* enough anticipation to quiet the niggling sadness that threatened to creep in when she thought of leaving Tom behind.

Her campus housing felt more like an apartment than a dormitory. She eagerly said her goodbyes, unpacked her things, and met her new roommates. Of the six girls, three were from Iowa, one from a town just outside Minneapolis, and she and another from North Dakota. Her new people.

Jeanie loved everything about the university. The smells, the sounds, the noise, the people. All of it. It was exactly what she had dreamed it would be. Her new adventure.

Throughout the fall, Tom visited several times, his eagerness to be with her outweighing his disdain for the big city. Unlike her, he didn't find it exhilarating and exciting. To him, it was loud, obnoxious, and curse-word provoking.

Because she had no car, they stayed connected primarily by exchanging letters.

Of course, Jeanie went home as often as she could. One weekend in October at his farmhouse, Tom knelt down on one knee and looked her in the eyes. "I want to marry you, you know."

Just. Like. That.

Jeanie knew it wasn't a formal marriage proposal, but the declaration made her heart flutter.

*I'm not sure we're ready for this*, she thought, a bit panicked. *It seems a little rushed.*

But she didn't voice her concerns.

Two short months later, somewhere along Interstate 94 headed east toward Minneapolis, Jeanie was telling Karen a story in the backseat of the family Pontiac. She gestured with her left hand to give emphasis to the story, momentarily forgetting to keep it hidden.

*Oh no! I hope she didn't see it!* Jeanie thought as she brought her hand back down. When Karen's eyes widened and her mouth formed a giant O, she knew it was too late.

"Holy shit!" Karen gasped in a hushed voice.

"What's going on back there?" Dorothy demanded.

"Jeanie has a ring!" Karen squealed.

"Howard! Pull over!" Dorothy screeched.

"What? Right now? What's going on?" Jeanie's dad grumbled as he maneuvered the sedan off to the side of the interstate.

Once the car stopped, Jeanie listened to her parents curse and scream like she'd never heard before. She sat in a dumbstruck silence as phrases like, "What the hell are you thinking? We told you to slow this down! What about school? What about your plans? He's way too old for you!" blasted with the heat and direction of perfectly executed missiles.

She didn't say a word. She'd never been the target of an attack like this. After all, she was their Good Girl. They never talked to her like this.

*It's not like I'm pregnant. I know I'm young, but aren't they being a tad ridiculous? It's not like I'm ruining my life. Maybe Tom should have asked Dad.*

Having the sense to never return fire, Jeanie silently surrendered. After her parents yelled themselves hoarse, they seemed to run out of ammunition. In the starkly grim silence, her dad steered the Pontiac back onto the highway toward Minneapolis.

When they pulled up to her apartment, Jeanie wordlessly exited the car, looking back at Karen, who gave her a tear-filled look that seemed to convey, *I'm so sorry, Jeanie! Please forgive me.*

Without any goodbyes, she walked away.

For the first time in her young life, Jeanie felt the raw sting of her parents' disappointment. She had upset them in the past, to be sure, but she had never felt such shame.

Later that week, she wrote them a letter attempting to express some of the things she had been feeling in the car and in the days and months prior to their explosive exchange. They had their chance to express their feelings. She took this way to express hers.

But two one-way conversations don't add up to one full blown two-way conversation. They never discussed it face-to-face again. It was settled, in her favor. Tom and Jeanie would get married.

## Lost in Translation

Since her plan wasn't to move back to Oakes, Jeanie was concerned about her ability to utilize the specialized degree she was spending both time and big money to obtain. She started looking around the area for jobs in the field she was pursuing and came up hopelessly short. In April of the following year, she left the hustle and bustle, exhilaration and energy of Minneapolis to work as a bank teller in Oakes and to prepare for her wedding and her future life.

Surrounded by friends and family, Tom Rodine married Jean Seefeldt in a simple, intimate service at St. John's Lutheran Church in Oakes on October 6, 1973. She was one month shy of nineteen. He was nearly twenty-seven. Although she hadn't planned to marry so young, she was blissfully happy to start her new life with Tom.

After a whirlwind honeymoon to Colorado to visit Karen, her best friend from high school who had been unable to attend the wedding, Jeanie caught a stomach bug. On her first morning of her new life as a farmer's wife, she was almost too ill to get out of bed. Without disrupting her, Tom rose early and went out to the field to combine millet.

Late in the morning, Jeanie wanted to fix him dinner, so she prepared it and left a note for him:

*Tom, I'm too sick to eat with you so I'm in bed. Your dinner is in the oven.*

*Love, Jeanie.*

At noon, she heard the back door open and listened to Tom bang around in the kitchen, comforted that he had a hot meal this first day home. Some time later, she heard a few more clangs and crashes when he put his dishes on the counter. The last sound she heard was the slam of the door as he shut it behind him.

Had he left really without checking on her? Was he mad? Jeanie worried that she hadn't met his expectations. *I bet his mother never missed a meal. I'm going to have to try to do better,* Jeanie thought. Her forehead slick with sweat from a fever and her body aching from the flu, her heart sank with pangs of discouragement.

The early days of adjusting to her new life as a farmer's wife were definitely a roller coaster—except she was in the back car all by herself and the ride wasn't purely entertainment. Jeanie couldn't anticipate what was coming next, and when she found herself in free fall, she had no one's hand to grab.

A city girl at heart, she was used to being surrounded by people. On Tom's farm she was alone from before sunup to after sundown with only brief reprieves at dinnertime.

It was as if marriage was a book whose jacket was printed in English, with a title and back cover promising romance, adventure, and a riveting storyline enhanced by glowing accolades from those who had reviewed it—yet, when Jeanie opened the cover to delve into the story, the entire text was written in Greek.

She needed a translator.

She knew she needed help, but she didn't know whom she could trust with her feelings. She didn't believe her mother could relate to what she was feeling, not that she'd have shared with her, anyway. Her pride kept her from unburdening her heart to the woman who lived her life under the guiding principles: *You made your bed, now lie in it;* and *Put your big girl panties on and deal with it.*

Plus, her marriage wasn't shaping up to be anything like her parents' marriage. Howard and Dorothy had a partnership in every sense of the word. Back in Wisconsin, Dorothy had worked right alongside Howard when he was a cheesemaker.

Not only did they work side-by-side, they managed their home as partners, too. Howard washed many dishes and changed at least a few diapers, not to mention the incredible challenge they had faced when Gary had his accident.

While they were certainly always respectful of one another, you knew where you stood with Dorothy Seefeldt. If she disagreed, even with her husband, she'd make her feelings known. She was frequently overheard saying, "I'll betch-ya!" when she was certain she was right. And that was most of the time. She stated her opinions as if they were facts. No, not just facts. Gospel truths. Delivered straight from the mouth of the good Lord, Himself.

The last thing Jeanie wanted to hear was, "I told you so."

After quitting her job in town, at Tom's insistence, to help him on the farm, Jeanie felt more than just lonely. She felt like a stranger in her own life. She thought about turning to her mother-in-law, Evelyn, as a source of support.

Evelyn was the consummate farm wife. She cooked meals for the slew of hired men who supported their work on the farm. She took lunch out to the field. (And, no, lunch wasn't the noon meal. It was a late afternoon snack consisting of coffee, lemonade, sandwiches, and some sort of baked good. Dinner was the noon meal and, typically, the largest of the day.) Evelyn did not purchase baked goods. She helped with the chores, mended fence, and was fully involved in the workings of the farm. She took care of the men.

Tom's father, Clifford, did not participate in anything related to the house, the cooking, or the cleaning. Every day at dinnertime, he sat in his easy chair, reading the paper while Evelyn prepared the meal. She would get the entire table set and chirp, "Clifford, come and eat."

He rarely responded to her first request. The first time Jeanie witnessed this, she thought he should at least acknowledge her after she had gone to so much work. Clifford was a stubborn Swedish farmer, and Evelyn was an accommodating farmer's wife. That was their way.

Jeanie couldn't fathom crying on Evelyn's shoulder. What would she even say? She tried to picture it.

"Evelyn, this isn't shaping up to be what I thought it would be. I didn't anticipate working on the farm. I don't feel like me anymore. Help me."

The thought was preposterous.

Jeanie expected a partnership with her spouse; Tom expected a traditional farmwife. Despite feeling somewhat lost in translation, they made a vow: They would lie in the bed they'd made … together.

## Searching for Purpose

To combat her loneliness and isolation, Jeanie started dreaming of starting her family. She had always wanted children and, while this was all happening faster than she had originally planned, she knew she would make a good mom. With children to care for, she would have purpose again. She would have value. She would have worth.

On November 6, 1980, in the local hospital run by Catholic nuns in Oakes, I was born. I arrived ten days late—proving that I would be nothing if not a headstrong child. According to my baby book, Mom and Dad selected the name Rebecca Jean Rodine because they liked it.

That's it. No family legacy to uphold. No real reason. They liked it. So they chose it for my name. Oddly enough, while they claimed to like it so much, my parents rarely called me by my full name. I was Becca Jean. Becky. Beck. Bunny. Bun Ellen Louise. Sissy. Sis.

My mom celebrated her twenty-sixth birthday two days later at a makeshift candlelight dinner with my dad and me—wrinkly, new, and helpless in the bassinet beside her bed. The hospital staff moved a little card table into her hospital room.

Mom was happy to have a birth experience worth celebrating. Her previous birth experiences hadn't been so easy. She had lost her first baby just four hours after delivery, due to severe complications in his development that, without the ultrasound technology of today, couldn't be detected until he was born. She never got closure with that experience. Birthing procedures of the day called for the administration of an inhalant that rendered her nearly incoherent when they first brought him to her in the delivery room. At the baby's funeral, she was not allowed to see him in the coffin. Her mother refused. Her father refused. Dad refused. They wanted to protect her.

But she felt robbed. She never got to see his face.

In 1978 while my parents vacationed with friends in Pelican Rapids, Minnesota, my older brother Joe—with little regard for timing—decided to arrive. He was born six weeks before his due date, weighing a little over four pounds. Medical staff insisted Joey stay until he reached a weight of five pounds. The hospital in Pelican Rapids had no long-term accommodations and my parents couldn't afford a hotel, so they returned to Oakes and visited Joe as often as they could.

Again, Mom felt robbed. Robbed of those precious early days to bond with her baby.

After they got him home, Joey suffered through several surgeries and complications due to his premature birth.

Being a chunky, healthy baby—and a girl—I was an answer to my mother's prayers. I was her miracle baby. When I arrived at the start of the winter season in North Dakota, she was more than content to stay tucked indoors, loving on Joe, snuggling me nonstop, leaving the farm only for necessary grocery runs and church services on Sunday mornings. She didn't want to share me with people. Permanently attached to my mother's hip, I was definitely a "mama's girl."

As much as she loved motherhood, after about a year home with me Mom needed something more to fill her bucket. She yearned for something of her own and to be useful to someone other than demanding, petulant children.

Four years earlier, Grandpa and Grandma Seefeldt had purchased the Ben Franklin store on Main Street. In 1981, Mom went to work for them. With a natural eye for design, she was interested in helping with merchandising. Grandma thought Mom should stick to doing books but, with some persuasion, she conceded and allowed Mom to do a little of both. Hurt that Grandma didn't recognize her value, Mom was determined to prove her wrong.

# Love Is a Battlefield

During the early 1980s, my parents' lives were a bit like a war. Two battles raged. Two chiefs battled on separate fronts. Neither communicated a strategy or battle plan to the other, but if either lost they'd both lose the entire war.

Chief Jean fought daily battles on the home-front with a headstrong, defiant toddler and a quiet, mother-pleasing older son who depleted her of all her available resources. She felt like a soldier fresh out of ammunition, hunkered down in a bunker, praying for enemy fire to stop.

Chief Tom fought the battle of his life to preserve the legacy of his family's farm. When Dad tried to renew his operating line of credit, his banker told him that the bank had devalued his entire net worth by half. His land, his cattle, and his machinery were all worth half of what they were before he'd walked through the door.

At this time in financial history, interest rates were 21% and net worth was king; banks did not lend money based on cash flow. Dad's net worth after the devaluation was $240,000 in the red. The bank would not renew his operating line.

In the resigned tone of a lender who had had one too many of these exact conversations, the banker offered, "Well, Tom, you have two choices. We can hold an auction sale, or you can ask your dad to come in and co-sign the loan for you."

Dad's chest fell. Although they still farmed together, the two had separated their finances years earlier. After a long minute, Dad took a breath just deep enough to puff it back up. "My father's got nothing to do with this. Get the auction set up."

Shoulders squared, he walked out of the office and climbed into his truck. They would lose the farm, their house, and all their belongings. The bank would sell everything.

All over the Midwest, conversations like this one were taking place. The pressure on bankers and farmers headlined stories about farmers committing suicide or, worse, killing their bankers and then taking their own lives. Thankfully, Dad did neither of these things.

He drove home to tell Mom he had lost his battle.

Later that week, the bank called Dad back for a meeting. After making their calculations, the bankers realized that, in even in the best case scenario, they'd lose nearly $150,000 on an auction sale. They made another offer.

"Here's what we'll do, Tom. We will shelf $110,000 of your outstanding debt and record it as a lien with the county. Then, we'll get you set up with Farmer's Home Administration. It's not ideal, but you can keep farming."

Dad had heard horror stories about working with FHA, but he knew he had no choice. In their first meeting, the FHA agent stated, "We will work with you for one year, with the goal to get you back in the black. Let's discuss your farm plan."

Dad's shoulders slumped. The particular horrors he'd heard all centered around farm plans. Because FHA was a government-run agency and received federal funding, getting their assistance felt a lot like being given a stick—a government-issued stick—and then being told precisely how to punish yourself with it. The "farm plan" was really more like using a crystal ball to account for everything you planned to use for inputs, like seed and chemicals, but you also had to attempt to account for machinery breakdowns. If your combine broke down and it wasn't in your farm plan, you received less funding.

In addition, Mom was required to list everything she planned to produce on the homestead. A detailed garden plan for FHA was probably filed away as some sort of an addendum to the farm plan proper.

The conventional wisdom, imparted by Grandpa Rodine, was to diversify. He thought it best to have a small operation of several business lines to ensure the farm was protected should one area crash. He chose not to "put all his eggs in one basket." The objective of diversification was to spread risk.

In Dad's mind, having pigs, cattle, and several crops of small grains simultaneously didn't really allow them to capitalize on the upside of spreading risk because of the downside of spreading their skill. The operation was too small to effectively manage all pieces of the farm. More importantly, the management skills required for small grain farming differed vastly from the skills required to handle livestock.

A handful of times, I accompanied Dad to his Aunt Marlys' farmstead where he raised dairy cattle. I'm not sure why I tagged along, because I mostly tried to stay out of the way. I can still smell the pungent odor of cow manure and feel the cold, dank pit where the milking machine was set up. I hated the milking barn. I think Dad hated it, too.

One bitterly cold December day as Dad was leaving, Mom reminded, "Don't forget. We have that Christmas party in town tonight with Mom and Dad, so you'll be done with milking by five, right?"

"Yep, I'll head over and start early. That should give me plenty of lead time."

When Dad pulled into Marlys' yard at a few minutes after three in the afternoon, all 150 cattle turned their heads, looking at him like they knew something was different.

*It's like the stupid animals can tell time*, he brooded.

After milking the full herd, Dad decided to get one last pregnant—and equally determined—cow into the milking barn. All of his typical tactics failed.

*It's like she's holding me up on purpose and doing this to spite me,* he thought. He couldn't get her to budge, which provoked a string of expletives vulgar enough to put a blush in the cheeks of the local bar patrons.

He finally resorted to an "unorthodox" method of moving her into the barn. He had started milking over forty-five minutes early. It took him over thirty full minutes longer than normal. He was late getting home. Mom was furious.

Dad wasn't in control of his schedule. Cows needed to be milked. He couldn't commit to be where my mother needed him to be. Cows needed to be milked. He didn't even like cows. And, yet, cows needed to be milked.

After years of heeding his father's advice and spreading risk through diversification, Dad finally resigned himself to the fact that he was not a livestock man. He got out for good in 1986 and put all of his eggs squarely in the basket of small grain farming. At least there was one less line item to put in the farm plan. One year with FHA turned into four, and Dad finally worked hard enough to become worthless. His net worth was back to $0.

Dad said those four years were the most soul-sucking, dignity-stripping of his entire career. Twenty years later when he wanted to buy Aunt Marlys' land, he had to clear the $110,000 judgment in order to finance the purchase. The bank had changed names several times during the years, and Dad knew they had written it off as a loss in the year they recorded it. Unsure what to do exactly, he asked the new bank president who said, "Make me an offer."

Dad offered $10,000 a year for three years. They accepted. While it wasn't even close to the full amount of the lien, they told him that of all the farmers they had done this for in the 1980s, Dad was the only one to come back and pay them anything.

Growing up, I knew my dad was a slave to his work, but I was blissfully unaware that not only were there Christmases where gifts weren't an option, there were several times during those years when Mom couldn't afford to buy groceries. It's amazing how great pretenders can shield children from harsh realities.

Mom, on the other hand, was never able to pretend away the truth: Dad had another wife.

She was high maintenance, impatient, and an insistent drain on Dad's energy and attention. For better or for worse, in sickness or in health, farming was the First Lady of his life.

After long days in the field, he would come home emotionally and physically beaten down by this abusive relationship. Meanwhile, Mom would want to share stories about her battle wounds from the day.

But she was not as demanding as Dad's first wife. Instead, she put on her big girl panties and did what needed to be done.

# Drama Queen

Calling toddler Becca Jean a "mama's girl" might be a serious understatement. "Mommy glom" is the phrase my behavior garnered early on and, truthfully, was a better fit. I loved my mother fiercely and, because she snuggled me nonstop for nearly a year, I grew pretty attached to her. This wasn't much of an issue until Mom started working in town and other people had to care for me.

When Grandpa and Grandma Seefeldt tried to hold or hug me, I ran from them, screaming like they were mass murderers. Grandma felt horrible. Grandpa thought I was a brat.

While slightly embarrassed by this emotional display, Mom secretly reveled in the fact that I loved her most.

That is, until I started to talk.

My mother often had things on her mind that she chose to not say aloud; I never held a single thought without verbally processing it. If it came to my mind, it came out of my mouth.

Mom only worked three days a week, and I'm sure that on some of her days off she yearned for the sun to burst through the next morning so she could have some peace. She probably felt more serene in a retail environment with customers than she did at home with a motor-mouth toddler.

I didn't just talk a lot. I felt a lot.

I was a highly sensitive and emotionally attuned child. I literally felt *all* the feels. They didn't even have to be mine and I felt them. Whether mad, sad, happy or glad, I felt emotions strongly and then wanted to *talk* about them. Can you imagine what a challenge this was for my mother? It wasn't long before my behavior earned me the label Drama Queen.

One summer, my parents hosted a barbecue with their best friends from church, Lyle and Noreen Hankel, and Pastor and Audrey O'Brien. Mom was preoccupied with hosting and didn't have much time for me. As the evening progressed, I felt less and less important and more and more hurt. After trying to get her attention for the thousandth time that night, I finally blew a gasket.

In an over-the-top, theatrical display, I hopped on my bike, toting my Going-to-Grandma's pink suitcase packed with only an extra pair of underpants and my toothbrush. I dramatically shouted through my tears, "No one loves me! I'm just going to run away!!"

The adults laughed until their faces hurt, listening to me bawl and carry on as I pedaled my little self down the road.

Good grief. They still mention this story to me. So maybe Drama Queen is a fair and equitable title. But, hey, even in the tough times I cared about my personal hygiene. That should count for something. However fair it might be, the label never felt quite right to me. It was as if being labeled a drama queen immediately discounted my feelings. Was it wrong to have strong feelings about things? Did feelings really serve no purpose at all?

I started to struggle with the big feelings inside of me. If I wasn't supposed to talk about them, how could I handle them?

## Family by Choice

As if growing up with two sets of biological grandparents wasn't fortunate enough, I had the incredible blessing of adopting a third set. Harvey and Ethel Karas were an older couple that lived just down the road from our family and looked after me and Joe during the summers while Mom worked at Ben Franklin. They were our family by choice. Not knowing any better, Joe and I called them Grandpa and Grandma. They never corrected us. They didn't yet have grandchildren of their own, and they treated us as theirs. It really was a win for both sides.

Their two children, Harvey and Jonda, were twenty-one years apart in age. Harvey terrified me slightly with his loud, booming voice and a presence that couldn't be ignored. But Jonda? Jonda was my idol. She was cool. She let me tag along when her friends cruised Main on weekends. In fact, she took her sweet time getting me all dolled up to show off to her friends; I was as necessary to her overall look as backcombing, banana clips, and a full can of AquaNet. I didn't care why she wanted to me tag along. I loved every minute of it and wanted to be just like her when I got bigger.

Every night, Grandpa Karas read his Bible aloud. When we stayed overnight with them, we sat at his feet and listened to him, capping the evening with "The Lawrence Welk Show." I wasn't thrilled by this nightly ritual and anxiously waited for it to end so I could eat whatever delicious treat Grandma Karas had made, not realizing I'd just devoured the best treat in the house.

The only thing Grandpa Karas loved more than Jesus was his bride and his children. And of course us—his family by choice. His deep affection for Grandma was evident by the expression on his face. Grandma Karas loved us fiercely and may have loved me a bit blindly. She quickly came to my defense if I did something wrong, usually with a treat in hand. I may have developed an overinflated sense of importance due to how special she thought I was, and I certainly developed a greater love of all baked goods because of her.

We celebrated nearly every major milestone with them, most importantly the shared birthday of Grandpa Karas and Jonda.

"More cake, honey?" Grandma Karas watched as I licked frosting—from my first helping of cake—off my fork. Without waiting for an answer, she piled more on my plate, and I caught the faint scent of bleach and yeast that Grandma's hands permanently carried. To Grandma Karas, no time was ever the wrong time for a treat. She was in her glory, hustling and bustling around their small farmhouse to accommodate the family who came to celebrate.

Shortly after we finished, Grandma declared, "It's time for presents!"

Grandpa sat at the head of the table. I hopped onto Mom's lap, directly across from him. After he opened a few, Grandma handed him our gift.

"We got you a shirt, Grandpa!" I proudly announced.

The room erupted in laughter. The whole room, except for me. I burst into tears.

I felt so silly. They were all laughing at me. I hated when people laughed at me. The rest of the afternoon, I couldn't shake the feeling that I'd messed up and made a fool of myself.

Grandma, noticing I was sad, leaned over and squeezed my cheeks. "Oh, Grandma loves you, honey." She handed me another treat.

# Mayberry

Living in the country forced me to be inventive and use my imagination to its fullest.

During the summers, I spent my days swinging from the augers parked in our yard, double-daring Joe to jump out of the hayloft, and creating an imaginary world in the old granary that served as my playhouse. Never wanting to hear my mother chide, "Only boring people get bored," I made sure to stay outside until mealtimes.

Unless it was literally too cold, which often happens in North Dakota, I played outside for much of the winter, too. I skated on the stock pond in our backyard, I double-dared Joe to put his tongue on frozen metal, and I sledded down the hills in the river valley.

With the exception of the Gebhardts who lived just on the other side of the shelterbelt to the south of our farm, our neighbors were more than a half-mile away in all directions. There was no such thing as a "play date." There was no such thing as being "overscheduled." I rarely was afforded the opportunity to swim at the pool in town. If it was hot outside and I needed to cool off, I had two options: the sprinklers or the cow tank. And, no, I didn't swim with cows. Geez. We weren't rednecks.

Going to town for ice cream—or anything, really—was a treat. And we didn't have treats every day. Unless, of course, I was at any of my grandmas' houses. Then it was an all-you-can-eat buffet of treats.

Besides playing with the Gebhardt kids, I also spent a lot of time at the Hankels' farm.

Lyle and Noreen had three sons. Shawn, their youngest, was closest to my age. Having no daughters of their own, they made me feel like a special young lady in their family, especially Lyle. He liked my dramatic spirit and could egg me on like no one else. My childhood is sprinkled with memories of Lyle and his sense of humor. I called him Fun Dad. He loved my spunk and my drama; I'm sure I was entirely tolerable in small doses.

I spent a lot of time at their farm, helping Shawn with the sheep. We rode on a trailer pulled by Lyle's tractor, singing loudly and making the chores fun. I didn't do livestock chores with Dad because it wasn't something he enjoyed. Lyle was a livestock man and his love for animals was evident. He taught me that hard work could be fun when you love what you're doing.

Shawn, too, had grandparents who lived across from them. One random summer day, we walked through the cornfield to his Grandma Hankel's house. After eating her homemade cookies and chatting, we knew it was time to leave.

"We're going the long way home," Shawn said. "We're going to walk on the road."

"Why?" asked Grandma Hankel.

"On our way here, the corn scratched our faces," I explained.

She immediately grabbed two paper grocery bags from the pantry, cut holes for eyes, and placed them on our heads. We giggled at each other but shot off full speed through the cornfield. Shawn's mom, Noreen, still laughs when she talks about seeing us come barreling out of the field with brown sacks over our faces.

It's hard to express what that kind of freedom, open sky, and country upbringing is really like. I guess you could say rural Oakes, North Dakota, was our very own Mayberry.

## Defining Cool

When I started kindergarten, the "city" kids attended half days. We country kids attended full days Monday, Wednesday, and Friday. I rode a bus to school until Joe was old enough to drive us. Although we lived only five miles from town, I had well over an hour bus ride on each end of the day. Our route picked up kids that lived nearly twenty miles to the west of Oakes.

That first day, I hopped off the bus in my blue and white dress, my hair fixed in what can only be described as a mullet without the business in the front or the party in the back. My straight hair curled under in a bob that ended a couple of inches above my shoulders— with bangs that went all the way back to the crown of my head. Mom curled and back-combed my bangs so the entire top of my head was feathered like Farrah Fawcett's hair, only much less "Charlie's Angels" style. Oh, and it mirrored my mom's hairdo, because that's what we did in the 1980s. We *matched*.

As soon as I entered the school, one of the teachers looked at me and observed, "You must be Jean Rodine's daughter. You look so much like her." I smiled. I was flattered. My mom was beautiful. I determined it must be my hair.

Having never attended a preschool program, I felt some anxiety about school. I didn't know what to expect, and I wasn't sure about the rules.

Although I didn't have class with the city kids, I did get to spend time with them on the playground at recess. They all seemed to know each other. The only person I knew was Shawn. Thank God, he was a country boy and we were in the same class. The girls talked about clothes and toys; the boys talked about toys and sports. I had never before given one thought to what it meant to be cool and just a couple of months of school had me questioning the right way to wear my hair and the cool stuff to have. I was no longer blissfully unaware of the things I lacked.

Suffice it to say, that Christmas of 1986—when my parents bought our very first Nintendo—was the highlight of my entire existence to that point.

Every year at Christmas, my cousins, Sara and Sadie (Karen's daughters), visited. If we were lucky, they stayed a few days. The girls, Joe, and I stayed up until we couldn't see straight, playing Duck Hunt and Tetris or hopping over mushrooms in Super Mario Brothers.

Sara and Sadie always seemed to get cooler stuff for Christmas. They lived right in Fargo; my mother managed a shopping trip there maybe two times a year, like the rest of our neighbors and friends.

After Christmas break, I had something relevant to discuss with my friends. I felt like I'd somehow arrived. All because of a Nintendo.

# A Brush with Rebellion

I loved the Ben Franklin store. The sights, the smells, the energy; it was such a magnificent store. And my grandparents *owned* it, which in my mind gave me social capital.

Grandma's office was in the back of the store where she did the bookkeeping. Every morning, Grandpa vacuumed the rugs in the front entrance and got the popcorn machine ready for the day. By the time I was old enough to visit my mom at work after school, she was managing the craft department.

During the1980s, crafting was the rage and Jean Rodine was the best in town. Through the years, she held Make-It Take-It classes in the store's basement where she taught people how to create wreaths, rag dolls, and Mod-Podge décor. A perfectionist, she lived by the motto: "If it's worth doing, it's worth doing well." Mom had extremely high standards and, on more than one occasion, had to fight the urge to tweak and perfect her students' creations.

Her original plan to work a few days each week evolved into less of a mindless escape and more of a vehicle to fuel her true passion. She never earned much more than minimum wage, but she loved having a creative outlet and supporting her parents' business. Finally conceding that Mom had real talent, Grandma was content to fully take over the accounting and let Mom flourish in her new role.

Located in the lofted balcony area, Mom's worktable was in the fabric department. A railing ran the full length of the balcony, allowing nearly a complete view of the entire store. I adored going upstairs to visit Mom. I would sit with a snack and my school bag, watching people as they came into the store. I also had a good view of the most beloved aisle in the entire store: the candy section. Mom's co-worker, Elaine, was in charge of the department and, boy, did I think Elaine was a star employee. I might have suggested Grandpa and Grandma give her a raise, she was that good at ensuring the kids of the Oakes community had a good selection of sweets.

One day after school, I had the urge to sneak something from one of the open bins that lined the bottom row of Elaine's aisle. I may have even felt a bit entitled to it. I chose a piece of gum and rolled it around in my hand. I looked up at the checkout area, back toward the other end of the aisle, and because of the bird's eye view it provided, did a quick sweep of the balcony. No one was looking.

*Who is it going to hurt? It's only worth five cents. Surely this store won't miss a five-cent piece of candy.* I quickly stuffed the bubble gum into my jeans pocket with a slight rush of shame, rebellion, exhilaration all rolled together. I knew stealing was wrong, but I justified that it wasn't a big deal. After all, it was practically my store.

Later that evening when I was getting undressed for my bath, the gum fell out of my pocket and bounced along the tiled bathroom floor. The sound caught Mom's attention and she saw me frantically trying to snatch it back up.

"Where did you get that?" she demanded.

Caught, I burst into tears. "F-from the store."

"What do you mean 'from the store'? Where did you get the money to buy it?"

"I-I didn't pay for it. I just p-put it in my p-pocket. It's only worth five cents." I cried pitifully.

Mom lowered herself to my level and, with hot tears of shame in her eyes, she said sternly, "Well, the way I see it, you have two choices. You can march your butt into the store immediately after school tomorrow and fess up to your Grandpa, or—you can go to jail. Now which is it?"

Jail? *I choose jail,* I thought. I knew the cops in Oakes. They didn't seem that scary to me. Grandpa was definitely scarier than jail.

"Well, what's it going to be?" Mom hounded.

"I guess I'll tell Grandpa about it," I said begrudgingly, knowing that was the answer she sought.

The fear and terror that gripped my heart kept me from sleeping more than a wink. While he certainly loved us, Grandpa Seefeldt had always intimidated me. He hollered when he was upset. He'd call us "dizzy shits" when we screwed up. He absolutely believed children should be seen and not heard. Frankly, he didn't want to see us, either.

After a full day in school barely paying a lick of attention to my teacher, I made the arduous trek of just over three blocks to the heavy, double glass doors of the Ben Franklin store. When I walked in, Mom looked down from her perch. She put up her hand as if to say, "Stay right there." I waited.

She grabbed my hand and marched me back to the office where Grandma sat at her desk doing bookwork. The brilliant smile she flashed at us disappeared as quickly as it arrived once she made eye contact with Mom and could see something was up. Grandpa was back in the corner at his desk.

"Becky has something she needs to tell you, Dad," Mom offered. I was already crying.

Grandpa walked over to stand directly in front of me. Grandma turned back to her books and pretended she wasn't listening.

"Well?" he huffed.

"I stole something yesterday!" I stuck out my hand with the gum in it, took a deep breath, and talked through my jerky sobs. "I brought it back and I'm sorry and I'll never do it again and I don't know why I did it and I know stealing is wrong and I'm so, so sorry."

Grandpa was angry, but he didn't holler or yell like I expected him to. All he said was, "If you want to come back to my store, you have to promise me you'll never do this again. Stealing's wrong."

I sniffled, "I know it is. I promise." And I meant it.

"You know, just because your grandma and I own this store, doesn't mean you do."

*How did he know I had thought that?* Eyes downcast, I nodded and shuffled away. Grateful for his merciful response, I vowed to never, ever again put myself in the line of Grandpa Seefeldt's fire.

## Disappointing Dad

One summer day, I rode my bike two miles down the gravel road to Grandma Rodine's farm where my dad was working on some machinery. Their farmstead had a looping gravel driveway that created an oval where the small red storage shed stood.

When I walked down to the Quonset where he was making some repairs, Dad looked up. "Do you want to take the three-wheeler for a little spin?"

*Why would I want to do that? I've only driven a lawnmower. I shouldn't drive a three-wheeler! Geez. What if I get hurt?* My thoughts ran wild. My inner perfectionist was afraid. I didn't *know* how to ride a three-wheeler. I had no desire to mess up and maim myself, but I really didn't want to let him down by being a wuss. After all, farm girls should be able to drive a motorized vehicle.

I hopped on.

He gave me a tutorial. "The brake is on the left and the throttle is on the right."

*That's it? That's all I get?*

"Just take her up the driveway, go around the loop, and come right back. Go slow."

*Go slow? You won't have to tell me twice!*

I started off. As my chubby little hand squeezed what I thought was the brake, the three-wheeler lurched forward and, with terror in my heart, I realized I'd already made a mistake.

"Dad!" I screamed as panic set in and the three-wheeler aimed straight at the red shed. "Dad!" My brain completely froze. So did my hands. I drove right into the side of the storage shed.

"Becky!" Grandma shrieked, running from the yard.

I did a quick self-check. A few scrapes and bruises, but I wasn't seriously injured. My ever-ready tears were from pure embarrassment.

Dad was visibly disgusted. "You had two things to remember. How did you screw that up?"

Grandma coddled me. "Oh, I'm so glad you're not hurt." She led me toward the house to soothe my mortification with a baked good. I glanced over my shoulder. Dad was walking the bent-up three-wheeler back to the Quonset, shaking his head.

I had not wanted to drive the stupid thing in the first place. Now, Dad was mad at me. *I always let him down,* I thought. *Maybe Grandma and I can talk about it.*

As we sat at the table, Grandma handed me a cookie she'd just pulled out of the oven. She never said a word about the incident. Neither did I.

## Motor Mouth

When I was in the third grade, our school implemented an after-school detention system.

A mere three days after the program started, I earned myself a spot. The system entailed getting your name written on the chalkboard after multiple warnings and a check mark behind your name for subsequent offenses, resulting in ten minutes spent in detention.

In class that morning while Mrs. Munsch covered a math lesson, I had leaned over to tell my friend a joke.

"Becky!" Mrs. Munsch scolded. "You need to follow along and be quiet, please."

She pivoted on her heel and proceeded to write my name on the chalkboard. Mine wasn't the first on the board that day, but it was my first time to be added to the list. Because the system had only been in effect for three days, my stomach sank at my teacher's disappointment.

Right before lunch, a similar incident occurred. I don't remember the details, but Mrs. Munsch gave me another stern look and warned, "If you're not careful, you're going to end up with a check mark behind your name. Is that really what you want?"

*Well, no,* I thought. W*hat I want is to go outside for recess where I can talk to my friends without getting into trouble.*

But I heeded the warning.

After lunch we headed to the library, leaving our building in a perfect single file. I slipped ahead about five students and popped into line behind my friend so I could talk to her. Mrs. Munsch was not pleased.

"We do *not run* on our way to the library! You just earned yourself ten minutes after school, missy."

My stomach knotted in fear and I fought back tears. *Oh. My. Word. My parents are going to be so disappointed in me!*

When we got back to class, Mrs. Munsch immediately walked to the board and placed that ominous check mark behind my name. I was so ashamed. Being a motor mouth was a bad thing. Being chatty landed me in trouble. I felt I needed to be different than I was.

I started wishing I was less visible. Less excitable. Less … *me.*

It was the first and last time I received detention.

## 4-H Fails

By fourth grade, I was finally old enough to participate in 4-H. Because my dad and animals didn't mix, I didn't join to show livestock. I joined because the Hankel boys were actively involved in our local club, which piqued my interest in the "arts" aspect of 4-H.

From demonstration exhibits to public speaking to submitting multiple projects in our county fair, I loved 4-H. I had an audience. I got to talk to people. I got to participate in competitions. It was a match made in heaven.

You would think having the goddess-of-all-things-crafty, the one and only Jean Rodine for my mom, I would have been a 4-H project frontrunner. Even though I loved making crafts, my execution was often subpar. While Mom never allowed a ball of dried hot glue or a drip of rogue paint on a completed project, she couldn't do them *for* me. She had to let me do them solo and stand in my own failures. And, boy, did I have my fair share of 4-H failures.

When I was twelve, "we" decided to do a demonstration in which I would dip-dye a woven basket. We arrived at the Ottertail Room, where our club's regular meeting and the demonstration competition were held, and pulled alongside the curb. As I unloaded the back of our car, I picked up the ice cream pail of dye, accidentally bumping it against the side of trunk. The lid popped off. Warm, red dye—with an artificial flower fragrance—poured down the front of my white tights.

Mom shrieked in horror and started shaking as she muttered curse words under her breath.

"I'm so sorry! It was an accident!" I said defensively, certain she was going to let me have it. Thankfully, only enough dye to ruin my outfit spilled from the container, so I was still able to do the demonstration, but she had to drive back home to get me a new outfit.

I especially loved the Project Expo. For this event, participants set up a tabletop tri-fold display board explaining their project.

*I've got this in the bag*, I thought as I walked through and sized up my competition.

My project was the creation of adorable watermelon cookies. Since the cookies looked just like watermelon slices, Mom and I designed the table in bright pink and green to match. We displayed the cookies on a round wooden plate that Mom had spray painted to look like a watermelon and applied a light coat of lacquer to give it a nice sheen. We set a full cookie jar off to the side of the plate.

When the judges came around to my beautifully displayed table, they questioned me about the project. I explained in perfect detail how I'd made the cookies. It was going swimmingly. Then, one of the judges picked up a cookie off the plate and took a bite.

The look on her face suggested the cookie wasn't good. She could tell from the earnest look on my face that I desperately wanted to win and so with grace and compassion, she choked down that bite of cookie, thanked me for my time, and moved along to the next display.

*What is going on? I know the cookie is nothing special, just a sugar cookie, and the real treat is in how they look. But, why did she make that face?*

As soon as the judges were out of sight, I grabbed a cookie and took a bite. It tasted like polyurethane lacquer. *Ugh.*

Mom sauntered over. "So, how did it go?"

When I told her the story, she wailed, "Why didn't you give her one from the cookie jar?"

"She just grabbed it so fast, I couldn't do anything."

Just like that, Mom's hopes and my dreams of winning were smashed like a ripe watermelon thrown to the ground. We had put so much effort into creating the perfect display and we missed the entire point: It doesn't matter how cute a cookie looks; it's not perfect if it's not edible.

# Hiding My Crazy

Sixth grade was the commencement of the toughest period of my youth, because I struggled so much with how I felt and how I looked. I couldn't articulate my feelings and, yet, suppressing them wasn't helpful either.

Dad didn't understand me. He thought I was entirely too high-strung about everything and that's how he dealt with me. He told me I was being ridiculous and sensitive. Plus, he was rarely home. He could leave when he had had enough.

My mom had to deal with me. When I had tantrums, she fled to her room with me frantically chasing her like a complete lunatic screaming, "I hate you! I hate you!" She would shut the door, a poor woman who simply needed a break from her touchy daughter.

In our family, we had an unspoken rule that you "hide your crazy" as if it's a slip under your dress that can tuck back in when it starts showing. This rule wasn't so much a function of putting on pretense; it was more about being private. But my crazy didn't tuck back in so easily. My slip was nearly always showing.

As a verbal processor, I found it decidedly difficult to fit into this mold. I always felt better when I vented my feelings. During this time in my life, however, I didn't share my feelings with anyone.

Unfortunately, sixth grade was also the year I participated in my first organized sport. Basketball. Most of the girls on my team had been playing since fourth grade, so I immediately felt out-classed. The larger problem was that I didn't understand the connection between failure and success. My inner perfectionist was embedded in my personality like a computer virus and I walked a wide path around screwing up and making mistakes. I didn't really see that it was a natural part of learning. But I was a tall girl. People expected me to play basketball. And kids with the "disease to please" do what they're expected to do.

Because I wanted to continue playing basketball, I endured my first sports physical in seventh grade. At the local clinic, I stepped on the scale, had my height charted, endured the medical routine. The nurse handed me my stats on a piece of paper. There it was, in black and white: I was 5'7" and I weighed 150 pounds. My eyes widened and my heart raced. *Well, that can't be right,* I thought. Most of the other girls in my class were just over five feet tall! They were infinitely shorter and lighter. Why did the nurse have to write it down like that?

One day as I walked to my locker between second and third periods, I reached around to scratch my back. My hand caught the edge of a piece of paper. I pulled, feeling the small tug of tape releasing from my shirt. "Wide Load" had been chicken scratched on the paper in black marker. I was shocked, mortified, and ashamed. Tears sprang to my eyes as I crumpled the paper into a ball and tossed it into the nearest wastebasket.

*Why would someone do that?* I hated being me. I hated being big. I hated whoever the jerk was who put the sign on my back. But, sitting around crying about it wasn't going to help. I held back my tears and told no one.

That night when I got home, my mom could tell something was wrong. I wanted to tell her what happened but she wouldn't understand. Mom was skinny. She had always been skinny. She didn't know what it felt like to be ridiculed and teased. I hated that I was so fat and she was my skinny mom.

Even though my adolescent heart desperately needed her, I shut her out. I buttoned up my feelings and tried to hide my crazy.

At school, I put on a happy face, making jokes and showing everyone what I wanted them to see. At home, I was bitter and angry. These years were brutal for Mom, too. She completely related to what I was feeling but she was certainly alarmed by how angry I was. She had serious concerns that this wasn't just a phase. That the bitterness, anger, and loads of backtalk were to be permanent facets of my personality.

While Mom spent her time searching for answers, I spent mine frantically searching for my big girl panties—and longing for baked goods. Take all the woes of junior high and sprinkle in the pressure of co-ed functions like dances … why, I just wanted to run away. And I'd need much more than what could fit in my pink, Going-to-Grandma's suitcase.

## Discovering Gifts

The fall when I earned my driver's license felt like a major coup.
I no longer had to sit for fifteen minutes every school morning while
my brother Joe performed his tedious pre-flight checklist. Now, *I* was
the driver. My parents let me drive a 1986 Oldsmobile Cutlass Ciera.
Fortunately, I was never a kid who cared about cars; I just loved
having my own wheels. Wheels gave me freedom; freedom gave me
options. I could pursue after-school activities. I could cruise Main
with my friends and offer to chauffeur them to neighboring towns
for street dances in the summertime. I could get a job that didn't
entail babysitting. I no longer need to rely on someone else to get me
where I needed to be.

At that time, we didn't have a formal drama club in Oakes, but
every year the Missoula Children's Theatre (MCT) would schedule a
week at our school. MCT offered a full theatre experience for school-
age children in the communities they served. They came into town
on a Monday, held auditions that afternoon and spent the remainder
of the week rehearsing for the performances on Friday and Saturday.

I auditioned for "The Pied Piper of Hamelin" when I was in first
grade. In spite of my nervousness, I got the part. I was cast as a rat.
I had no lines. I was the equivalent of a choral member, a choral

member in a rat costume. I soaked up the energy. I loved the whole process.

I had participated in every play they offered, but now I felt like I was getting too old. And by old, I mean that no one really thought plays were cool. I didn't want to be lame, so I quit.

The best part of these plays was that they were musicals. I truly loved music. Grandma Seefeldt had given me a year of piano lessons for a birthday gift when I was six, and while I didn't always love practicing and loathed recitals, I loved the instrument and continued with lessons through high school. And, paying some sort of homage to my lead singer, guitar playing, record producing dad, I also loved singing.

I felt alive when I had an audience. The challenge of garnering a smile or a full belly laugh because of something I did or said was like a drug to me.

My last role as a freshman was the unfeminine, sporty, wicked stepsister of Cinderella.

In one scene, the wicked stepsisters belittled and bullied Cinderella at her big debut at the ball. Cinderella (my friend Sarah) stood front and center stage. The other stepsister (Jessica) and I stood behind her, against the backdrop. We weren't scripted for this part of the play.

As soon as Cinderella got to her mark, I mocked her loudly, saying in my macho voice, "Really? Look at that dress. Pink and blue? Together? Tacky. Hideous!"

When the scene ended, I went backstage. Smiling broadly, two directors pulled me aside. "We were dying of laughter back here! We've never heard anyone ad lib that scene as well as you did! If you haven't considered pursuing acting yet, you really should. You have a gift."

*A gift? Well, who knew I had a gift for acting?*

That kind of feedback from two people I respected thrilled me to the core. Sadly, I had already made up my mind to quit. I cared too much about what peers might think of me to continue something that I not only enjoyed but, apparently, had a *gift* for.

Thankfully, many of my cool friends liked music as much as I did. If letting go of plays felt like losing an appendix, letting go of music would have felt like cutting off a limb. Our high school choir was good and Oakes was known for being one of the top choirs in the region. The show choir provided the community with a music and dance performance—a "café concert"—each spring. The director selected the music, but the students were largely responsible for the choreography. We provided over an hour of entertainment of singing and dancing in hideous, matching sequined outfits.

It was glorious.

We competed twice, once when I was a sophomore and once when I was a senior, at a large-group music festival in Branson, Missouri. The competition was fierce and we got a taste of what large schools probably had for an operating budget in their music department. We sat in awe when one of the largest schools performed a number where a girl skated on an ice rink in the center of the stage.

"This is like a Broadway show!" we whispered to each other as we watched with our mouths hanging open.

When it was our turn to perform, we just walked on stage and sang. No hubbub. No extravagance. Definitely no ice-skating. While we probably should have been embarrassed by how little we did in the way of performance comparatively, Branson was a great experience and we were proud of what we'd done.

While we were there, a waitress asked if we had running water and electricity in North Dakota. Really? One of my friends replied, "Nope, and it was a really long ride down here on horseback."

My best friend BJ and I hatched a big plan (well, let's call it a half-baked plan) to start a band of our own: The Water Buffaloes. Truly gifted, he went on to play with a well-known regional band; I sat in my room with dreams of our fictitious band touring the world.

My athletic career was less than stellar. I worked hard but, truthfully, my mental game was lacking. No one ever told me I had a gift for athletics. Although I loved playing basketball, I felt too much pressure. I'd rather be alone on a stage singing than having a full team of girls and full stands of our community members relying on me.

Despite my late start and admitted shortcomings, when I was a junior our team won the 1997 Class B North Dakota Girl's High School Basketball Tournament. We actually *won* the state tournament. Our combined record for my sophomore and junior years was 52-1; we lost just one game in two full seasons. If you want to see small town spirit at its finest, watch a town follow a winning sports team like ours. With school closed the Thursday and Friday of the tournament to allow students to attend, there was hardly a soul left in town. In addition to our team bringing home the title, our community, who filled the stands with a sea of orange and black, also won the Spirit Award.

Being part of that team was a tremendous gift even though basketball didn't fuel my passion. I was grateful for all the lessons that I learned on the court, lessons that I could apply to real life. Mostly, I was grateful to live in Oakes, where a kid could explore all of her interests without the added pressure of having to be the best at everything. Explorations allowed me to learn.

I started to come into my own. I shined the brightest when I was working. At fifteen I landed my first real job. I had loved the families I babysat for, but to be clear, I was no young Jeanie Seefeldt. I craved adult interaction and never felt like a nurturer. I started working as a waitress at our local diner, The Main Street Café. I topped off the mugs for local coffee groups, delivered glasses of milk *with the meals,* and learned the valuable lesson of serving others— even when they might not have deserved the nicest treatment.

I quickly realized that I was an asset in the workplace. I was a dependable, hard-working, quick study. I was mature but still brought fun to work. In fact, that was my unique and valuable contribution: I made work fun.

I felt needed. I felt valuable. I felt the most like *me* when I was working.

And while I always got a deep sense of satisfaction from my jobs, I wasn't one of those kids who always knew what I wanted to be when I grew up. My mom may have experienced an intuitive hit about what I would do for a living. She returned from an event in town one evening and couldn't stop talking about the speaker. *My mother couldn't stop talking?*

"I was so inspired!" she exclaimed. "I really think you could do that job for a living."

"What job?" I asked, with more than a small amount of curiosity.

"You could be a motivational speaker!"

"Uh-huh. Sure. And what exactly would I talk about?"

"I don't know," she admitted. "I just feel like it would be the perfect fit for you."

*Okay, Mom, I'll be sure to sign up for Motivational Speaking 101 when I go to college,* I silently sassed.

## **Nestie**

In the winter of 1999, a businessman from the Fargo area—with roots in Oakes—opened a business called Performance Centers, Inc. (PCI), a telemarketing firm. Once basketball season was over (back when girls basketball was played in the fall and the world made sense) and spring rolled around, I was ready to find a new after-school job. I had quit the restaurant the prior spring and worked as a lifeguard and swimming instructor that summer. While my job at the pool never paid more than minimum wage, $5.15 per hour, PCI offered $7.50.

That was *big* money to me.

With visions of new Girbaud jeans dancing in my head, I applied for a job. Because it was one of the best paying jobs in the area for high school students, many of my coworkers were from nearby towns. This allowed me to feel free in this job. My typical shift was from 4-7 p.m. on weeknights and then a full day on Saturday.

While lunching in the break room, a handful of us started a spirited discussion about the hit television show, "Saved by the Bell." I stood in front of my new friends, doing my best impression of a specific dance involving the character Lisa Turtle. None of us could remember what the dance was called. A tall, slender girl with glasses walked over and inserted herself into the discussion by saying, "It's the sprain. That dance was called the sprain." And she danced alongside me.

*Who is this?* I wondered, with not a hint of jealousy. She was hilarious.

"Hey, I'm Becky," I said after our impromptu performance.

"I'm Missy. I just started working here. I drive from Hecla with Emily and Andrea." I knew Hecla was—even by Oakes standards—a tiny town about twenty miles south, just inside the South Dakota border. When she mentioned that she actually lived way out in the country and was driving nearly forty miles each way to work at PCI, I knew it was fate that we'd met. It certainly wasn't coincidence.

"Well, you do a mean sprain," I teased.

"You should see my impression of Jessie Spano when she overdosed on her caffeine pills," Missy said with a grin.

Simultaneously, we started singing "I'm So Excited" by The Pointer Sisters in the same way the character, Jessie, sang in her room when she was hopped up on today's equivalent of speed. We smiled knowingly at each other. It was settled. We would be friends.

My tenure at PCI was admittedly short because I was leaving for college in the fall, but I would never have lasted as long as I did if it weren't for Missy. We brought the same asset to the workplace: we made work fun. The job itself was appalling, but we had some hilarious moments together. We relayed the comments we'd received on phone calls, and people said some really awful things. Missy placed a call once to a southern guy and in the middle of her pre-approved credit card spiel, he suddenly hollered, "You people are nothing but a bunch of shit-eating mosquitoes!" and hung up on her.

We spent one whole break devising a response and actually placed several calls trying to imitate his southern drawl. Yes, we placed calls using fake accents. Maybe I wasn't always dependable, mature and responsible, but the job was fraught with verbal insults from callers. If we didn't make it funny, we would have spent our shifts crying.

Sitting in our cubicles with our headsets on, we'd make calls with the press of a button on our computer screen. One beep and we knew the call recipient was on the line. After a two second delay, the recipient's name appeared on the screen, giving us no time to consider its proper pronunciation. Once, I heard Justin, who sat across the aisle from me, slowly and painstakingly attempt to pronounce a name.

"Hello, Mr. Ni-goo-an? Oh, I'm sorry, Mr. Ni-guy-an?"

I couldn't hold back my giggles. As soon as the guy hung up on him, Justin turned to me and Missy. "So, how would *you* have said this name?"

"Spell it."

"N-G-U-Y-E-N."

Laughing in spite of my efforts to rein it in, I said, "Oh Justin, it's Wen. That name is pronounced Wen."

"Well, how am I supposed to know *that*? Man, I suck at this job!" Justin did, indeed. But really, who of us didn't? And, furthermore, who would want to admit they were good at this job?

If Missy was my first lifesaver, the handheld mute button was my second. In the middle of a call, particularly one where either the other party was getting angry and hostile (like Southern mosquito guy) or Missy and I were trying on a new accent (perhaps a lisp), we'd have to resort to continually pushing the mute button throughout the call to keep the person from hearing us laugh.

I was my authentic self around Missy. She was the first friend I ever had that I showed all my crazy to—and she loved me anyway. In fact later that summer, our church youth group had an outing planned to Duluth, Minnesota. I asked Missy to join us. It was only a couple of days away, but she immediately ran to our manager to ask for the time off. I accompanied her for moral support.

Jen shook her head with regret as she consulted the schedule. "Oh, Missy, I'm so sorry. With Becky being out and a few other planned absences, we really need you to stay here and cover the floor."

Missy looked at Jen like she had just taken away her birthday. Forever. "So, you're saying I can't go?"

"I'm sorry, but no, I can't let you go." Jen sounded slightly irritated that she had to actually state the obvious.

"Well," Missy extended her hand to Jen, "it's been nice working for you."

*What the hell is she doing?* I wondered.

As I stood beside Missy with my mouth agape, Jen simply shook Missy's hand with a look that seemed to say, *I can't believe you're doing this. This is pathetic and you are silly.*

We punched out for the day. Before we had even left the building, I started laughing. Uncontrollably laughing. "I can't believe you just quit your job to come on vacation with me!"

"Well, this trip better be fun," Missy said, with her deadpan humor. "Who else can say they quit their job for you?"

"No one. I doubt there will ever be another person for the rest of my life that will be able to say that, Missy."

Up to this point in my life, I had had basketball friends, church friends, 4-H friends, and music friends. Friends who fit into categories based on the common experience or hobby we shared. Missy was the first person I formed a friendship with who transcended that history. With her, I didn't have to compartmentalize the facets of my personality or my hobbies or my interests. I could just be Becky.

As my closest confidante, she became the first to call me out on my B.S., and the one I turned to with good news and bad. Nothing in my life felt real until I shared it with her. I knew friendships like this were sacred. She was "in the nest" with me. I called her my "Nestie." At eighteen, I was finally bold enough to be myself—and blessed to meet a friend that accepted me just as I was.

At a telemarketing company in rural North Dakota, I found my first Nestie.

## Young Love

According to an African proverb, "It takes a village to raise a child." Well, my parents certainly had a village. I didn't even try to get away with much. I was too afraid of the village to stray from the good-girl lane. I had three sets of grandparents plus church families to help keep me in check. Why would I even bother?

Like other small towns, Oakes was intimate, which is probably a nicer word than most would choose. A person couldn't even get a speeding ticket without gaining notoriety. Our local newspaper published the Dickey County Sheriff's Report. We considered that *news*. It wasn't really public shaming; they printed it because they could. Word of my misdeeds got back to my parents faster than I could drive my sorry butt home. And, for some reason, the idea of partying in a cornfield never appealed to me! So, I didn't drink (a lot), I didn't do drugs, and I didn't sleep around.

I worked. I played basketball. I studied hard. I participated in school sanctioned activities. I went to church on Sundays. And I always needed to have a boyfriend to break up the monotony of that goodness and create a little drama in my life.

Toward the end of my basketball career my senior year, a friend approached me after a game and told me that a particular boy in my class wanted to ask me out.

*You're shitting me!* I thought. *Why on earth would he be interested in me?*

I'd always thought the boy was cute, although completely and totally not my type. He was a jock and always dated cute girls that were jocks. You know, cute, *small* girls. The kind of girls that would look good with him. Even after I lost my baby fat, I was always a little too large to carry off the adjective "cute."

I was kind of freaked out. I didn't get it. In fact, I had been hoping to re-ignite the former flame of our sophomoric relationship with my future Water Buffaloes bandmate, BJ, picturing our ability to tour the world as a couple, a more modern and hip Sonny and Cher. Our fans would love that we were a couple. Alas, my hope for our paired musical stylings was unrequited; BJ had his eyes on someone else. Someone admittedly cuter but much less musically gifted.

The fact that so many girls had loved the same guy—a complicated, ugly situation in a small school where we recycled boys among us—and he was interested in me, oddly made me feel special. We started dating just a few weeks later.

Our high school romance was fraught with the typical B.S. of most high school relationships. Because I was still overly conscious of my slip showing, I didn't let him all the way into my heart. We lacked shared interests and thought differently about the world. The thing that hooked me though was that he always made me feel like he needed me, which ignited my savior complex. I always felt this strong responsibility to protect him from himself. I adored his family and, on more than one occasion, his mother said, "We're so blessed you're with our son."

My disease-to-please kicked into high gear, and I chose to focus on what I brought to his life instead of what might have been missing from the relationship, not a great long-term relationship strategy.

# Koree-with-a-K

The pit in my stomach grew larger and larger as the distance to Jamestown College (JC) grew smaller and smaller. Mom and I were on our way to check out the housing situation.

As we strolled the campus, she commented, "Jamestown is really beautiful. The buildings seem to have so much history and the grounds are stunning. Look at those amazing lilies. My lilies struggled this year. I wonder what kind of soil they have here?"

Barely listening, I was busy worrying and wondering about the roommate I'd been assigned from the two thousand enrollees. Oddly, perfection-seeking, Type-A personality Becky Rodine had left her roommate situation to *chance*. After we'd been informed of our pairing, Koree and I had exchanged several letters over the summer, but this was our first face-to-face encounter.

*I can't believe I allowed for this,* I thought. *I don't leave things like this to chance. What if she was a psychopath? Or just not funny? Or what if she were super cool and thought I was the lamest person she had ever met? Why hadn't I just chosen a roommate from one of my classmates?*

Of my forty-seven high school classmates, seventeen were attending JC, a private institution a quick eighty-five miles from home. I had been awarded the Presidential Scholarship, which paid half my tuition.

"You can't waste an incredible opportunity like that," my dad had said. "What smart person would turn something like that down?"

So I enrolled. Like a smart person should.

Mom and I entered the courtyard on the west side of Kroeze Hall, the dormitory where I would be living in just a month. We went up the concrete steps, opened the heavy glass door, and entered, greeted by the scent of Musty Old Apartment. I located my room, the first door on the left in Section B.

"This is it? It's so tiny. And cold. And sterile."

"Oh, don't worry," Mom assured me. "We'll find ways to punch it up."

I turned at the sound of a light rap at the door. A girl with short blond hair smiled brightly, brushing her bangs to the side. She put out her hand. "Hi, I'm Koree. It's nice to finally meet you."

Noting her firm handshake and confident eye contact, I immediately sized her up. Koree was tall, almost as tall as me. She wore a butterfly necklace, pale pink cardigan, and black skirt.

She was cute. She seemed articulate and well-mannered. So far, so good.

"Did you look at the dressers in the closet yet?" She interrupted my silent assessment. "I think they're from Ethan Allen."

*Seriously? She noticed that? Is this some kind of joke? I love that she's noticed that!*

In one step, Koree crossed the room to our beds. "What do you think about putting one underneath the other, like this?" She moved a bed frame so it was perpendicular to the one on top. "Then, I thought we could coordinate our bedding so it looks like we planned to live here together."

*Be still my heart. Was there some type of roommate proclivity assessment that I took without remembering? How did they know to pair me with this person?*

Mom exchanged a quick look with me and it was settled. Koree was a fit.

As we climbed back into the car that afternoon, Mom turned to me. "Koree. That's an interesting name for a girl. How do you spell her name?"

"Oh, it's Koree. With a K." I snapped my seat buckle. From that point forward, that was how my family referred to her.

Koree-with-a-K became my second Nestie.

## Becoming Rebecca

Shortly into my first semester at JC, I felt a strong impression that I wasn't supposed to be there—even though Koree's presence served as a continual reminder that I'd never find another roommate as perfect as she was. My boyfriend was a factor, to be sure. He was attending school over 145 miles away. A big chunk of my heart went with him. And, with so many of my high school classmates around me, it felt like round two of high school.

I wanted to meet new people. Experience new things. Be on a bigger campus. So after just one semester with Koree, I left the quaint, cozy campus of Jamestown College for the hustling and bustling, *huge* campus at North Dakota State University (NDSU), which had an enrollment of ten thousand—five times the population of Oakes!

I moved into an apartment off campus with one of my high school classmates, Katie, who had also transferred to a school in the Fargo area. Eagerly, I dove into my new field of study, interior design.

To make ends meet, I got a job as a hostess at the local Olive Garden, where I mastered the art of necktie tying and perfected my rendition of the Italian birthday song, forever etching the words in my memory.

When I moved back home for the summer, I spent a lot of time discussing the future with my boyfriend, certain we were meant to be together. He wanted to return to Oakes and support his family's business. We spent long summer evenings dreaming over a book of log cabin house plans. I was totally unaware that my mom got a pit in her stomach every time she saw us looking at those plans. It terrified her to think I, too, might marry young and abandon my education. Of course, she never said those thoughts aloud.

When it dawned on me that interior design was an expensive and useless degree in Oakes, I reluctantly switched my major back to business administration, assuming it was marketable enough to find employment even in my tiny hometown. I tried to ignore the resentment that gurgled inside me.

When I started my classes that fall, I moved off campus to an apartment by myself. For the first time, ever, I spent a decent chunk of time alone. While it was slightly isolating, I learned to sit with my feelings. And I had plenty of time to ponder my situation.

*Did I really want to live in Oakes? What would I do for work? Could I be happy there? Was the idea of moving back to Oakes really the problem, or was I using it as an excuse? Was I really happy in my romantic relationship?*

When I got tired of ruminating, I hung out with new friends I'd made in school or drove to Wahpeton to visit my boyfriend in the apartment he shared with my cousin Sara, who was working in Wahpeton while her boyfriend, Nathan, another of my high school classmates, finished school. We knew they were on the fast track to marriage.

Those weekends were part of the reason I hung onto my relationship as long as I did. When the four of us were together, time stood still. There was no expectation to move forward; we could be eternally stuck in high school. I loved how natural and comfortable it felt.

When I wasn't in school or socializing, I was working. That fall, I landed a steady job in the department store at the local mall, selling high-end clothes in The Oval Room. The kind of high-end that I shouldn't have been touching let alone selling. If Mom thought I had expensive taste before …. After paying rent and expenses, I flashed my employee discount and spent every red cent on clothes—not the clothes in my department; even with a discount, they were way out of my budget.

On my first day, I checked in through the employee entrance and they handed me my nametag: Rebecca. I had never gone by my full name. It wasn't a mistake *per se*; they had simply taken it directly from the legal name on my application. A little jarred, I pondered the idea. *Should I say something? Should I ask them to change it?*

I decided to try it on—the nametag and the fancy name. And, just like that, I became Rebecca.

## Meeting Michelle

I was growing as a person and started to like the new me, name and all. As my world expanded, I realized I didn't want to freeze time. I wanted to change, learn, and grow. I could love my past without making it my present. And certainly not my future. I wanted out. After more than two years together, hundreds of great memories, and countless explosive fights and heartaches, it was time for me and my boyfriend to part ways. The weight of his parents' disappointment felt palpable. Although they never said a word about it, I felt I'd let them down.

When summer arrived, I was thrilled to stay in Fargo. I moved into an apartment south of NDSU's campus on Dakota Drive with Michelle, a girl I met in my first interior design class a semester earlier. Of all the seats in the auditorium, I had sat next to Michelle. Several times, I caught her looking at me as if she thought she knew me.

"Were you Player of the Game? In the 1997 State Class B Girls' Basketball Championship Game against Hazen?" she finally asked.

Was she a stalker? She hadn't missed a beat in that string of words. "Um, yeah," I replied, dumbfounded.

"You're Becky Rodine, aren't you," she said, more statement than question.

It was surreal to be recognized from basketball. I mean, it wasn't even one of my *gifts*. "Yeah. And you are …"

She chuckled. "Michelle. Nice to meet you. I'm from Beulah, an hour north of Bismarck, just a dot on the map. We went to the tournament to cheer for Hazen. I remember you because you shut down Hope Shied and no one had ever done that before."

Michelle was a sports fanatic. Clearly. After that initial conversation, we became great friends. We both spent only one semester in interior design; she switched to education with an emphasis in physical education, perfect for her.

With a great job, a fun new roommate and no boyfriend tying me down, I felt free to do whatever I wanted. And apparently I wanted to partially make up for staying so squarely the-good-girl-in-high school. I didn't become a pole dancer, heroin user, or take on any other role that would warrant shock or disgust. I was underage at the time. I partied—a bit less than a lot. I partied … moderately.

Every bad decision I made my last years of college involved Michelle. I think her parents held out hope that I'd be a good influence on their wild, reckless, adventure-spirited daughter. After all, I was the good girl who made smart decisions. I'm thankful that Michelle's personality won out.

## Liquored in Lilac

"Shot?" Koree asked as I pushed a stray bobby pin back into my updo.

"Like you have to ask?" I countered. "Make it two! We can't spend time trying to down beers every time we come back here. We'll get full and it takes too long."

She smoothly filled two clear plastic cups one-third full with vodka and handed one to me. "To Sara and Nathan. To dancing. And to having fun without boys!" Koree held up her glass to mine.

"Cheers!" I said as we clinked and downed the contents. The slow burn of alcohol warmed my throat and belly as we sauntered from our hotel room to make our way back to the reception hall.

I quickly spotted my cousin Sara in her candlelight white wedding gown, my fellow bridesmaids in their lilac dresses, and the rest of the women in my family on the dance floor. Koree and I ran out to join them. Several dances later, we were doing our own rendition of the Macarena, which involved me bending all the way over to the ground and shaking my rump in a circle at each refrain of "Hey Macarena!" After the third repeat of the chorus, I dizzily tried to stand upright. The vodka had caught up with me.

Slipping away from the dance floor, I took a seat at a nearby table and held my spinning head against the heels of my hands. How many drinks had I consumed, anyway? I had no idea.

Koree appeared at my side. "Are you okay?"

I slowly shook my head. "I'm heading to the restroom."

Koree went into best friend mode, grabbing a glass of water and some napkins and followed me. I stumbled into the first stall and sat right down on the floor. As my stomach churned, my mind started to wander and the tears started to flow.

"I just don't understand how we got to this point," I slurred. Koree nodded sadly and rubbed my back. "Having to see him all day and walk down the aisle with him was just so hard," I moaned. "I am so mad at myself. I know I said I didn't want to be together, but I miss him. I think I still love him. And now I'm drunk and I'm crying. Why do I have to be such a mess?"

As those last pathetic words rolled out of my mouth, so did the contents of my stomach. I threw up a few times, laid my head right on the toilet seat and let the tears fall.

The bathroom door flew open. "Becky!" Mom's whisper was frantic. "You need to pull yourself together. Your grandma's coming!"

There was no door on the stall where I sprawled. I looked at the billowing satin of my lilac dress. How on earth I was supposed to pull myself together? There was no hiding. There was no tucking in this crazy. It was literally bursting under the walls of the stall.

When the door opened a second time, I knew Grandma Seefeldt was in the bathroom. I was ashamed and fearful, wondering what she would think of me. I lifted my head and glanced over my shoulder as Mom attempted to block the doorway with her tiny size-eight frame, trim in the sharp little suit she wore. She was trying to hide me.

"Mom, you don't want to look in there," she pleaded.

Grandma stood on tiptoe to peer over my mom's shoulder. Her face fell. To my surprise, she didn't give me a look full of chastisement or disappointment. She appeared empathetic. Understanding.

"Oh, Becca Jean," she murmured in compassion.

Whatever façade I planned to uphold crumbled with those three small words. I dropped my head back to the toilet seat and sobbed. I cried because of a boy. I cried because I was missing out on Sara's party and I loved Sara like a sister. I cried because my grandma's love overpowered my shame.

After I had no tears left to cry and no food left to vomit, I felt ready to leave the bathroom. I was escorted back to my room by Koree on my left and Grandma Seefeldt on my right. They helped me undress and tucked me into bed, where I drifted into foggy-headed sleep, comforted by the knowledge that I was loved. In spite of me letting my crazy show.

# Serendipity

After a year of proving myself in The Oval Room, I advanced to the granddaddy of all department store positions. I found myself working for commissions at the Estee Lauder counter. Instead of high-end clothing I couldn't afford, I now sold high-end cosmetics that I also couldn't afford.

I learned some valuable skills. From the people who tried to return products clearly not purchased from our store, to the *man* who sat down in my makeup chair because he "was hoping for a few tips and tricks to keep his makeup in place," I found myself in unexpected situations where the customer was clearly *not right*. I had to smile and figure it out. *Oy*. Working in retail forced me to become skilled at working with people. And I really became good, which freed me to speak easily to strangers.

Strolling home from class the second week of my junior year, I crossed the T lot on the south end of campus on a sunny afternoon. I noticed a fellow weaving around cars in the parking lot. Although headed the same direction, we completed our bob and weave strategies on opposite sides of the street. I looked at him and smiled.

"It seems we're going the same way," he said.

"It sure does," I replied. "I live on Dakota Drive. How about you?"

He pointed to the little house directly in front of us. "I live right here."

"Well, maybe I'll see you around sometime."

"Sounds good." His response left me hanging and we went our separate ways.

The following week, he came up behind me as I crossed the lot. "Dakota Drive, right?"

I laughed. "Well, hey. Our paths cross again." He fell into step with me. "So, where are you from?"

"Jamestown originally."

"Really! I attended Jamestown College my first semester." I liked this new connection. "Maybe we know some of the same people. What year are you in school?"

"I'm a freshman this year."

Because I had more college under my belt, I doubted we had mutual friends. "I'm a junior but, well, there was a girl from Jamestown who lived in my dorm. Her name was Keri. Keri Smith."

His eyes widened. "I know Keri." His voice dropped to a murmur. "I dated her."

I nearly stopped in my tracks. Earlier that summer, Keri had visited my apartment on Dakota Drive. Koree happened to be staying with me that weekend. We hadn't seen Keri all summer so we chatted the night away and, of course, had a few too many drinks. And when I say we, I mean Keri. Keri had too many drinks. She told us she'd been dating long distance because her guy, JJ, was in the military. Now that he was returning to North Dakota, she was terrified he wouldn't like her anymore. Neither of us could believe that. Keri was gorgeous, with a bigger-than-life personality. But her face had broken out a bit and she was afraid he'd be turned off by the blemishes.

As good friends do, I had tried to comfort her. "Well, what kind of an asshole would dump you for that? It makes no sense. You're worrying over nothing. I can't wait to meet this guy. You talk about him like he's incredible."

Keri looked at Koree. "Well, you can meet him." Her head swung in my direction. "But you can't."

My brows shot up. "Why can't I meet him?"

She shrugged, lowering her eyes. "Because he'd probably fall in love with you."

Now here I was, standing with this guy in the T lot. There was a strong possibility …. I squinted up at him. "What's your name?"

"Jeremiah."

"Do you ever go by JJ?"

He was obviously surprised. "Um, yes."

"Did you just get back from North Carolina because you were stationed there with the military?"

"Well, yes." His jaw tightened and he eyed me with suspicion. "How did you know that?"

He looked me the way I'd looked at Michelle at our first meeting. *Oh no, he thinks I'm a stalker.* A nervous giggle escaped when I cautiously admitted, "I feel like I know all about you."

We walked a few more blocks while I explained. Inwardly, I was stunned. What were the chances that I'd randomly meet the same guy that a friend told me would be perfect for me?

I went straight home and barreled into the apartment, startling Michelle. I told her the whole story finishing with, "Wouldn't it be crazy if I were to marry this guy?"

# Uncertain Times

Two weeks later, I was sitting in my 8 a.m. finance class when our instructor informed us a plane had reportedly flown into one of the buildings of the World Trade Center just fifteen minutes earlier while we strolled to school. A New Yorker by birth, he proceeded to draw us a fascinating map of downtown Manhattan. He repeatedly reassured us that it was likely a small plane, but we should wait to learn more.

After class, I walked to Memorial Union where I saw a crowd of about forty students hovered around a TV. The news outlets were live streaming and I could see that it had not, in fact, been a small plane. I sat down cross-legged on the floor among the other students. At 10:03, we all watched in horror as the media provided live action of the second jetliner as it barreled through the South Tower of the World Trade Center.

We sat in stunned silence.

I had never been to New York. I didn't have family or loved ones living there. But that didn't matter; this was happening to my country. My people. On American soil.

Fear gripped my heart. My breath caught in my throat and I barely noticed the tears streaming down my face. Although most of us were strangers to each other, I didn't feel alone. As we tried to wrap our minds around the unimaginable, the girl sitting next to me reached over and gripped my hand. Riveted and unnerved, we finally grasped that we were witnessing an orchestrated attack on our country, involving other planes with other targets.

We watched the South Tower collapse fifty-six minutes after the original impact.

Two days later, I met up with Jeremiah on our way to school. In the couple of weeks since we first met, we had walked to and from our classes as often as our schedules allowed. He was now serving in the North Dakota National Guard and, with the attacks on our country, was concerned about getting called back to active duty. We sat in the fall leaves of the front yard of his house, which we simply called "1042," and talked about life. I never had conversations like this with my high school boyfriend. But Jeremiah and I could maintain meaningful dialogue for hours. He was smart and kind and those traits made him fiercely attractive.

My mind was probably in love with Jeremiah before my silly heart—which still pined for my ex—caught up. With all the uncertainty swirling around our country, I yearned for things safe, comforting, familiar. And who was more familiar than my first love?

## Gasping for Air

Shortly after turning twenty-one in November, I drove home for a weekend. After eating supper at Grandpa and Grandma Seefeldt's house, I went to a party at my ex-boyfriend's apartment in Oakes, hoping the two of us could talk. Secretly, I yearned for reconciliation. The partygoers were a mix of guests much older than me and, of course, a few from my class who were still under the legal drinking age. When there was a threat of police crashing the party, I hid in a closet with a high school classmate. Because of some rough patches in our friendship, I hadn't seen her for several years.

Once the threat of being busted subsided, she pulled me aside as we left the closet. "I know this seems strange coming from me, but there are a few things you should probably know."

She shared a detailed accounting of my ex's "extracurricular activity." I was devastated yet grateful she told me the truth. Then, embarrassment reared its head. How many people knew about this? Everybody but me? Was I the only one in the dark? I felt so stupid.

I gathered the last shreds of my dignity and marched up to my host. "It looks like we have some talking to do. Why don't you come out to the farm when you're done here?"

As I drove away, I felt a need to talk this out with someone else. But not my mom; I wasn't ready for her to know. And not a classmate; at this point, I wasn't sure who I could trust. When I got home, I raced upstairs to my bedroom, picked up my flip phone, and called the one person I knew I could tell: Jeremiah. As the phone rang, I prayed he'd answer.

"Hello?" His sleepy voice made me glance at my watch.

"Hi, it's me. Becky." My own voice sounded feeble.

"What's wrong?" He suddenly sounded wide awake. Concerned.

His easy compassion touched my heart as much as the fact that he could tell in my voice that I wasn't okay. I blubbered and told him everything.

I had never before fully given my full heart to anyone. Call it protection, call it a safety net, call it my family's way, but whatever the reason for holding back, I made it impossible to be completely known by anyone.

"You're the total package, Beck," he said.

"What are you talking about?"

"You're beautiful and you're smart and you're a really good person. You don't deserve to be treated like this."

Didn't I? Maybe there were things I should have done differently. Maybe I should have given more of myself to the relationship. Maybe I shouldn't have constantly thought about how we weren't a good fit and focused on what we did share in common.

My emotions had calmed by now. "Thank you for listening. I appreciate it so much."

We said our goodbyes and I went to sleep, grateful for our late night talk.

After church the next day, my ex-boyfriend called my parents' home number. We agreed to meet later at the farm. When Mom started prepping supper around 4 p.m., I asked, "Can I talk to you for a bit?"

"Sure." She scrubbed at the dirt on the potato she was holding, not even looking up.

I climbed onto my perch on the countertop, where I'd watched Mom cook since I was first old enough to sit. I began telling Mom what Sarah had shared with me the night before. Mom was visibly shocked. She and Dad had loved him like family, and she obviously felt as betrayed as I did.

My tears had escalated to the kind of sobs that are almost primal in nature by the time he walked in. He stopped midstride and looked at us, faced with double the anger, double the hurt, and double the disappointment. If looks could kill, the poor kid would have died on the spot.

We went outside to his truck and talked. I shared what I knew and pleaded with him to explain why. He offered no excuse. No reason.

Perhaps, deep down, he knew he'd committed the unforgiveable and, in doing it, managed to free himself from my impossibly high expectations. I knew I was not an easy girl to love. Maybe he was tired of feeling never good enough.

After he left, I went back into the kitchen where my mom waited. "I've been thinking about this, Beck. You are never going to be able to let this go. I think you have to give this relationship one more shot. If you don't, you'll always wonder if you made a mistake."

Despite all her concerns over the years about us looking at house plans, changing my major to fit in Oakes and the possibility of an early marriage proposal, my mother had never dispensed advice. And now, her suggestion was to stay in the relationship?

*What? Why would you want me to be with someone who doesn't really love me?* But, deep down, I knew Mom was right. Mom knew I needed to feel like I'd given it my all.

It only took two months. On Valentine's Day when he came to visit me in Fargo, we both knew it was time to end the relationship. We were not meant to be together. Why did it take me, the smart girl, so long to figure this out? I still felt like I was letting down his family. Yet this was an important lesson for me to learn: you can't save someone who doesn't want to be saved.

And you can't save someone if your own plane is going down. I couldn't stay in a situation that deprived me of what I needed, simply to please someone else.

I needed to secure my own oxygen mask.

## Family-Tested, Nestie-Approved

A week later at NDSU, Jeremiah came over to study with me.

He looked up from his textbook. "I've liked you since the moment I met you. I'd like to take you on a real date."

My heart fluttered with excitement as he finally verbalized what I felt I already knew. We went out for drinks and dinner that Friday. That's when I knew. I finally trusted him enough to let him all the way in. I trusted him with my whole heart. My dramatic, spirited, slightly crazy heart. Had that been the only test, he'd have passed with flying colors. There was one more test to pass. He had to meet "my people."

The first opportunity arose a month later. Koree planned a weekend visit to Fargo and I was anxious to introduce her to Jeremiah.

"If you don't like him, I won't keep him," I promised in a phone call, giving her the ultimate power to squelch the relationship. It could have been a showdown of epic proportions.

But they were fast friends. Jeremiah understood what Koree meant to me and she had a hunch he'd one day be my husband. He tolerated our inside jokes and just rolled his eyes the time he walked in on us snuggling on the couch watching *Steel Magnolias*, weeping when Sally Field broke down at the graveside. He had been deemed acceptable by one of my Nesties.

Missy, the Nestie who quit her job for me, was in South Dakota attending college, so she supported the relationship from a distance. A real Nestie did that sort of thing.

Easter weekend, we decided to roll the anxiety of meeting parents into one trip. Jeremiah was the first boy I dated where I had a meet-the-parents experience. I already knew the families of local boys I dated, so this was unnerving. We drove to his parents' house in Jamestown on Friday, and I put my best face forward. I was quiet, kind, and well-mannered, just like Mom had taught me to be. Jim and Teri Undem seemed pleased enough with our first interaction. With that stress-bomb out of the way, I was excited to properly introduce Jeremiah to my folks. Mom had briefly met him in passing one time when she visited me in Fargo. She knew the important role he'd played in helping me find my way back to myself, so I was just ready for them to know him like I did. I had developed a wonderful relationship with my mother, in particular, at this point in my life, but my dad was also a ton of fun. I really expected Jeremiah and my parents to hit it off.

I did not expect to witness what my parents had planned for our arrival.

As we walked up the steps in the garage to the door, I lightly knocked to give them a minute to compose themselves.

No one answered.

I knocked a little louder and waited. Still, no answer.

"Well, this is weird," I apologized. "Mom's car is here and Dad's pickup is outside, so I assume they're home." I cautiously opened the door. "Helloooo? We're here!"

I turned toward the sound of rustling in the kitchen and see a bright fuchsia pump emerge. My mom stepped into full view. I gasped. My mouth fell open.

Mom wore a bright floral dress that *she made* in 1988 for Harvey Karas' wedding. The tufted shoulders and fitted bodice crowned a voluminous, tea length, A-line skirt. The aforementioned pumps had been dyed to match a bridesmaid's dress worn at Jonda's wedding several years later. On Mom's head perched the blonde wig that Audrey, our pastor's wife, had occasionally worn when battling breast cancer.

*What the hell?* I tried to make sense of what I was seeing. *She looks like a deranged Stepford Wife. What is going on?*

Enter Dad. He wore a ten-gallon hat with a brown corduroy jacket—and held a shotgun.

*What. The. Hell.* I was so bewildered that even my thoughts repeated themselves. *My parents have completely lost it.*

I had no words to sputter. If their only aim was to totally and completely surprise me, they nailed it. Tom and Jean Rodine for the win! I glanced at Jeremiah who simply stared, his bright blue eyes widened like saucers. Obviously, he didn't know what to think, didn't know if this was normal for my family.

My mother started talking in a fake, high-pitched voice that was half defective Southern drawl, half bad British accent. "I was just pulling the pie out of the oven. I'm so glad you kids are here."

I burst out laughing. They burst out laughing. Poor Jeremiah was not laughing.

I was so thankful his parents had just opened the door and welcomed me into their home like perfectly normal human beings. Mine had to flaunt some crazy.

Easter was one of the holidays when former classmates returned home and celebrated with nights out together. I would drink too much, stay out too late and, in the morning, crawl my hungover rear out of bed to go to church. For sunrise service. At 7 a.m. no less. Because that's what good girls did. Jeremiah, on the other hand, was always a responsible drinker. I don't know whether it was the pressure, my dad's shotgun, or if he just really enjoyed the taste of his Jack and Cokes that night, but he overdid it.

When we pulled into the yard around 2:30 in the morning, he didn't want to come inside because he knew he was going to throw up. He thought it more discreet to hurl outside. Unfortunately, he puked into my mother's rose bushes, near their open bedroom window. So much for discretion.

Easter belonged to Grandma Seefeldt. At dinner, Jeremiah got to try his hand at impressing my entire extended family. Other than being hungover and really, really tired, his first family gathering went off without a hitch. Grandma was smitten with Jeremiah when he complimented her coconut dessert.

"I'm not much of a sweets kind of guy," he said, "but, Dorothy, this dessert is amazing."

The jury was in: Jeremiah had passed the family test. We were keeping him.

## A Diamond in the Snow

On December 17 of my senior year, I had tried all day long to reach Jeremiah. The weather was nasty and I was concerned that something had happened to him. Finally, he showed up at the back door of the house I shared with Michelle and two other friends. He seemed edgy and evasive when I asked him where he'd been.

"Will you come with me somewhere quick?" he asked.

"Really? I'm wearing a tank top and sweatpants. I'm all ready for bed." I gave a sigh of resignation. "Where are we going?"

"Oh, you don't need to dress up. Just throw on a coat and come with me."

"But, it's really nasty outside and I have a final tomorrow. Can't we do it later?" I whined.

"Oh, good grief. You're ready for your exam. You're always ready for your exams."

Shrugging, I tugged on my boots and threw on my winter coat, hat, and mittens. *This better be worth it,* I thought. I hopped into Big Red, the manual transmission, Chevy S-10 truck, which Jeremiah had bought while living in North Carolina and was sorely unsuitable for North Dakota winters; it slid around like a pig on ice. He pointed the truck west. I could feel his nervousness.

The realization of what was happening dawned on me when he pulled into the open, barren T lot on the south end of NDSU's campus. My heart raced.

Jeremiah stopped at a specific point in the lot that held special meaning for us. "Will you get out with me?"

I didn't hesitate. I asked no questions. I nodded and hopped out.

There, with snowing swirling in Big Red's headlights—at the exact place we'd first spoken to one another—this sweet North Dakota boy with piercing blue eyes and remnants of a North Carolina accent, got down on one knee. He opened a little navy blue box.

"Beck, I loved you from the first moment we met right here in this spot. Will you please do me the honor of becoming my wife?"

I squealed with delight and practically tackled him to the ground. I loved the ring and I loved the way he asked me.

When we got back into the truck, he looked like himself again. "Where have you been all day?" I still buzzed with excitement, but was too curious not to ask.

"I drove to Oakes to ask your parents if I could marry you."

"In this blizzard? That's insane!"

And it was. He could have gotten into an accident. But I was proud of him. Of all the things he'd gotten right with this proposal, I was most thankful he'd asked them. This meant my parents were pleased.

## Finding My Groove

On October 4, 2003—10-4, good buddy—two days before my parents' thirtieth wedding anniversary, I became Mrs. Jeremiah Undem. The intimate service at St. John's Lutheran Church in Oakes landed on a simply perfect fall day. Friends and family surrounded us.

Jeremiah was a good man. Marrying a good man was always part of my plan. I can't say that I had ever specifically uttered the words, "I'll *never* marry a farmer," but I certainly hadn't planned to. And Jeremiah didn't plan to become one.

Because of his five-year military stint right out of high school, he had a few years of an undergraduate degree yet to complete. The burden of supporting our new household fell on me.

There was incredible opportunity for upward movement with the department store where I was still manager of the Estee Lauder counter, but I couldn't see myself staying there. I didn't want to spend my life working weekends, and I was tired of arriving at 5 a.m. on Black Friday.

I'd always felt kind of silly saying, "I work in the mall," when people asked. It seemed like a temporary college job. Me, I had aspirations of climbing a shiny corporate ladder.

Once the focus of wedding planning was behind me, I applied to *all* available jobs in the Fargo-Moorhead area. I opened the classifieds and put in my application for any job that required someone with a business degree. Did I give one thought to what I *wanted* to do? Of course not. I needed a job that paid the bills and, hopefully, offered some benefits. I'd work hard and climb wherever I landed.

When I saw a listing for a Human Resources Generalist opening, I called my friend Kelly, who was an executive assistant to the CEO of the well-respected, fast-rising manufacturing company in Fargo.

"I love working here and I highly recommend them as an employer," she said to me on the phone.

I applied the next day and as soon as the interview was scheduled, I purchased my very first black business suit, determined to "dress to impress" as I'd learned in my business classes.

Nervous, I smoothed a sleeve as I sat in the nice conference room, waiting for the CEO to arrive.

*I'm nailing this interview,* I thought with satisfaction toward the end of our conversation. That's what I did. I nailed interviews.

His eyes narrowed. "How do you think you'll handle working with all these men on the manufacturing floor?" He didn't wait for me to respond. "In this role, you'll be interacting with them a lot, and I think they'll find your good looks and stature to be too intimidating. I don't think they'll find you approachable."

It sounded like his mind was made up. He wasn't going to hire me. He apparently believed my height and, I guess, *femaleness* to be a problem.

*Kelly is way cuter than I am!* I thought indignantly. *Have you looked at Kelly lately?*

Defeated, I left the conference room, the shock of the reality setting in. I had never experienced this before. I had been offered every job I'd ever applied for. This was a blow to my confidence, a blow to my ego. I went home and cried to Jeremiah. I might have consumed a baked good or two.

Eventually, I got a lead on a position in the loan processing department for a regional bank. The mother of one of the women who worked at the Estee Lauder counter for me was the HR director of this bank and since she knew I was looking to leave retail, she passed the information along. Ironically, of all my college courses, I got my worst grade in finance. Consequently, banking never interested me. But, hey, they liked me enough to hire me and they offered a decent starting wage.

I loved working in downtown Fargo. I loved that our building was shiny and corporate looking. I loved that I rode an elevator to the fifth floor of a building to get to work. Even though I was working in a cubicle, I felt like my job *mattered*.

Because of my inexperience in the banking world, I threw myself into learning. I caught on quickly. It was new. It was interesting. And I was fortunate to work for a company that valued me as a person. I was soon promoted from the operational side of the bank to a client-facing role as a personal banker. I had my own office, with a real door and a window that looked out on the world.

After a successful year of securing valuable friendships and business partnerships, and meeting the challenge of acquiring federal licensing, I loved my job. I felt valuable. I felt needed. I felt like *me*.

Our bank ran advertisements with our photographs in The Fargo Forum of Fargo-Moorhead, so many Oakes friends commented when I returned home for weekend visits. My parents were so proud of my accomplishments that they had a bouquet of flowers sent to my office for my first anniversary there.

My coworkers were like family. We spent a lot of time together outside of the office, playing coed softball in the summers and frequenting local watering holes to sing karaoke. Even though we didn't see a lot of each other with Jeremiah still in school, our marriage was solid. We had purchased our first home with my newly learned knowledge of mortgage lending.

Our home life was great. I had meaningful relationships with people I cared about. I was climbing the ladder in a rewarding career. My life was unfolding just as I'd planned.

*I had found my groove.*

Through my job, I often attended personal development seminars and workshops. I would always come back to my office with ideas about how to incorporate things I'd learned into our branch location. The first time this happened, I was reminded of something my favorite university professor said to me. Dr. Ramaya, who taught the capstone course of the business administration degree, was tough and quick to challenge students publicly. Many of my peers loathed him. In his Strategic Management class, we reviewed a lot of case studies and ran mock companies. He engaged us in vibrant dialogue about what we read and challenged us to look beyond the numbers presented in a case study.

"The people matter," he would say. "Culture isn't about just strategy and execution. It's developed through courageous leadership."

In short, he was the professor who had the biggest impact on the trajectory of my career.

I had numerous conversations with him outside of class, too. One day, I stopped by his office to discuss a project.

"What are you plans for employment after college, Rebecca?"

I shrugged. "I don't really know."

"May I give you a piece of advice?"

Counsel from a man I admired? "Sure!"

"You are one of the brightest students I've seen when it comes to engaging in critical thinking and dialoging about your thoughts. You have a gift for interpreting company culture unlike what I typically see. You should pursue your MBA and consider becoming a business consultant. It would be the perfect fit for your skillset."

*Wow. Dr. Ramaya thinks I have gifts!*

At the bank, my coworkers and I held daily meetings (we called them pow-wows) to talk about culture and attitudes. I was unintentionally using the gifts Dr. Ramaya first mentioned. But my job at the bank was to close loans, find new clients, and take care of existing customers. It's not that this newfound passion wasn't needed or wanted by my employers; it simply didn't mesh with what I was paid to do.

For the first time since starting my job with the bank, I questioned whether this role was right. What if this was all there was? Could I be happy doing this forever?

# The Undems Go West

Thankfully, I didn't have to make any decisions about staying or going. When Jeremiah graduated with his degree in landscape architecture and natural resource management, he was offered a job in Billings, Montana. When he hesitated to accept, I thought he didn't want to deal with the hassle of moving.

"This is a great opportunity for you. We should at least entertain the offer, don't you think?"

Later that month, the firm flew us to Billings for a visit. Jolene, the principal agent and owner of the company, seemed nice and took time to show us the pertinent things. Jeremiah's prospective office was nice. Billings was close in size to Fargo.

*This could be the start of a new adventure for us!* I thought. Throughout our trip, I tried to gauge his interest, but he gave nothing away.

On the flight home, I finally asked, "So, what do you think?"

"I just don't know if I'm going to like this kind of work."

"The only way you'll know is to try it. Sometimes, the best lesson is to learn what you don't want," I said, thinking I sounded wise. Truthfully, I feared he would never take a leap of faith on anything. Jeremiah was cautious and analytical. I gave him a gentle nudge.

It was settled; we were moving. I would leave my job because I had to, not because I wasn't sure it was a fit. The idea of starting fresh was exciting.

Before our senior year of college, Koree-with-a-K, who had always wanted to become a nurse, decided to join the Navy. When she followed her dream to sunny San Diego, I was thrilled for her. I was also a tad jealous. I envied people who always knew what they wanted to be and pursued their dream. I couldn't believe she had the courage to go out on her own and leave everyone behind. It seemed so cool and adventurous. Brave, even.

Montana was no California, but it was a start.

Leaving my coworkers and the job I loved so much was as hard as leaving family behind. Then, there was my actual family. Moving away from my parents was hard, but I had the toughest time leaving Cousin Sara behind. She and Nathan had their son Tyler just six weeks before our wedding. He was the first baby in our family and we loved that little guy so much. We spent many weekends at their place, playing cards and drinking beer. Gone were the days of going out to paint the town, and we wouldn't have wanted it any other way.

The night before we left for Montana, I hugged Sara on the street outside our empty townhome. Tyler snuggled in his car seat. I couldn't even look in at him without feeling my heart rip apart.

The next morning, family gathered around us in our driveway and Jeremiah's dad, Jim, said a prayer for our safe travel to Billings, asking God to guide our ways in our new home.

We could have rowed our way to Montana in the river of tears I shed.

# Battle Cry

We pulled into Billings, tired but happy to have arrived safely.

"Well, I guess this is it," Jeremiah said as we entered the main office to meet the landlady of our furnished apartment. We had rented the place sight unseen, planning to stay only until I found a job and we located a permanent home.

Jeremiah used the key we'd been given and turned the knob, pushing open the door to our new digs. But there wasn't even enough clearance for the door to swing all the way open. The door opened into the bedroom, which boasted less than a couple of feet of walking room all the way around the bed. I walked in.

You could've sighted a shotgun straight through to the kitchen and out the door on the other side of the apartment. And you could almost check the roast in the oven while sitting on the toilet. It was the tiniest apartment I'd ever seen, less than three hundred square feet.

"It's a good thing I really like you," Jeremiah quipped.

"There's no one else I'd rather be stuck in this tiny apartment with than you, honey," I replied.

We unloaded our few belongings and called it a day. I sighed and looked around. "At least it's really clean."

Jeremiah started work the next day. I set about the task of finding a job and a house.

This would have been a great time to explore different career avenues, but because my professional experience had been mostly in financial services (and I was still trying to do the smart thing), naturally, I applied only to the banks in town. As I scheduled interviews, I worked with Judy, our real estate agent, to find a home. We knew we wanted to live in the area of town called The Heights, located over the rock formation known as The Rims that surrounds the city of Billings. The Heights offered a more spacious feel than other neighborhoods, and on clear days you could even catch a view of the Rocky Mountains to the west. Of course, all of that came with a price tag. It wasn't more expensive to buy there, but the commute into the business district, while scenic and beautiful, was the longest from any neighborhood in town.

I accepted a job as a personal banker with a big box bank. My starting salary was about $10,000 less than I made in Fargo, but I figured with all that upward potential, it would be fine.

The possibilities seemed endless and I was ready to explore them all.

When we closed on our house, a large bi-level in The Heights that needed more than a little love, I immediately called my parents so they could bring the truck out with our furniture. Thrilled to help me set up house, Mom squealed with delight. I could hardly stand the wait.

As I stood in my new kitchen with its drab but solid wood cabinets, I decided we should perk up the kitchen before my parents arrived with our stuff. I had to gently nudge Jeremiah on the idea of new flooring. We installed it together, and we didn't kill each other.

Our teamwork wasn't always pretty, but the flooring sure was. We updated the wall color and I got to work on the cabinets. I decided to paint, antique, and distress them.

After removing the twenty cabinet doors, applying three coats of paint and one application of rubbed-out stain to every part of the cabinets, I finally finished them. My hand was cramped into a claw from holding a paintbrush, but I'd made my goal. Each time I considered quitting, I thought about my mom saying, *"Just put your head down and keep going. You're not a quitter."* It worked every time.

The evening when Mom pulled into our driveway and Dad parked the semi on the street in front of the house, I felt like the world made sense again.

When I bragged about the cabinets, the look on Mom's face gave her away. She was worried about my execution. She walked into the kitchen and gasped. "Becky! Look at these! They look amazing! And the wall color! And—did you guys install this flooring yourselves?" She absolutely gushed. I had done it! I executed a DIY project that met my mother's expectations! Take that, 4-H fails!

Mom and I made quite the team. In just one short week, we transformed that place into a home. Warm and cozy. We discovered Granny's Attic, a three-story warehouse store filled to the brim with antiques and repurposed furniture and home items. We brought boatloads home with us. Even though we were exhausted, we had a blast.

When it came time for them to leave, I wasn't ready to let them go. Dad got on the road early since he was driving the truck back. I clung to my mother like a toddler, only wiser, knowing a tantrum wouldn't keep her there. When she climbed into her car and looked up at me one last time, I broke down. I felt like she had taken my beating heart right out of my chest and strapped it into the passenger seat beside her.

We liked living in Billings. The city was great. The weather suited us. It snowed. It melted. It melted because it didn't stay cold long enough to keep the snow on the ground. This was a novel concept to us North Dakota natives. We'd found a lovely church and met some really amazing people. The trouble was they weren't "my people."

My fondest memories in Billings centered on the times our family came to visit. Nathan, Sara, and Tyler arrived in September, announcing that they were expecting again. As I threw my arms around Sara, it dawned on me that we didn't live in Fargo anymore. We would barely know this child. We hosted Jim and Teri for Thanksgiving. We hosted my parents for Christmas. Jeremiah's brother, Seth, and his future wife, Laura, visited the following January to ski at Red Lodge. Koree made a trip out to celebrate her recent engagement to Jason, a fellow Naval officer. The adventure of living away from home felt thrilling when sharing it with family.

But, on a day-to-day basis, I struggled without them. When Mom mentioned in a phone call that the family was getting together to celebrate Grandma Seefeldt's birthday, I winced with pain. I hated that I couldn't run home at the drop of a hat. I hated living so far away. It just didn't feel right.

Then there was the issue with our jobs. Neither of us enjoyed what we did. Not even a little bit. If I felt uncertain before about fitting with banking, this new position confirmed it. In my previous role, I was free to be outside the office, meeting with new prospects and networking. I managed a loan portfolio and earned lending authority, making it possible for me to do my work without asking anyone for approval.

In my new job, practically none of my skills were utilized because, frankly, the job didn't require them. I was overqualified. I had my first taste of what it's like to work for a big company. I struggled with the environment, was insulted by bureaucracy and, moreover, hated the feeling that no one ever questioned why things were done the way they were. Although I appreciated the shiny buildings and the incredible systems, I didn't care for this newly found revelation that I was just a number.

My rebellious spirit emerged and she was not happy. I cried on my way to work four out of five days every week, especially the first few months. I felt like a little girl who, on Christmas morning, got exactly the gift she'd been yearning for since she first wrote her Christmas list: the Barbie Dream House. She'd dreamed about it, thought about it would look when she got it, pictured how perfectly happy and forever contented she would be to play with her Barbie Dream House. Then, after a few weeks of owning it, she realized it was not as amazing as she pictured it. She quickly tired of it. Even with all the bells and whistles it offered, she thought it could be better. Her dream didn't match the reality.

The reality of working for a big company was so much less grand than I'd pictured.

Jeremiah's hunch about his job was right all along. He didn't enjoy the work. When I saw how unhappy he was, I wanted to fix it, fix him. I researched other options for him in his field. When I provided at least two solid ideas in Billings, he shook his head.

"Those jobs will be no different from what I'm doing now," he said. "I don't know that I enjoy how design-heavy these jobs are. I don't want to be stuck behind a desk all day."

"What do you want to do?" I asked. "What kind of jobs should I start looking for?"

"I really didn't want to come here to begin with." He dragged out the words with reluctance. "I miss our families. I want to be back in Fargo."

I let that realization sink in. Apparently, my gentle nudging had felt more like shoving to him. "Why didn't you say something? I would have listened."

"You had your mind made up about coming out here," he pointed out. "I moved away when I was eighteen. I thought you deserved your moving away experience."

*Well, that's kind of sweet,* I thought. Still, did he really not want to come out at all? Was I to blame for the move to Montana?

"That was generous of you. It really was. But if you had serious doubts, you should have said something. This is supposed to be a partnership. And the reason I pushed so hard was that I wanted you to find contentment in your job like I had." I paused in reflection. "That sure backfired! Now we're both miserable."

Only then did I recall a lesson I thought I'd learned: I can't save someone who doesn't think he needs saving.

"From now on, let's vow that we'll talk about all of our feelings on a subject and, even if we know it might hurt the other person, we'll never move forward with a major decision we're not both fully supportive of."

"Sounds good," Jeremiah said.

I offered our battle cry. "Team Undem?" Early on in our marriage, we'd promised to not rely too much on the opinions of outsiders like our parents when making decisions. We made decisions as a team.

"Team Undem," he confirmed.

We lived in Billings for a little less than one year before we returned to Fargo. While we were there, Jeremiah discovered he couldn't work at a desk. I discovered I couldn't work for a big company. But, like I told him before, sometimes you can't know how you feel about things until you try them out.

## Snark and Sass

Back in Fargo once again and still reeling from the disappointment of my big bank work experience, I was too scared to search outside of what I knew and decided to return to my former employer. It was safe. It was familiar. It was comfortable.

I started intentionally networking. By intentional, I mean I'd had my fill of going to events, meeting new people, and getting a purse full of business cards but still leaving with an empty heart. I was tired of the forced and phony exchange of business cards. I wanted to meet *real people*. An acquaintance suggested I attend a particular all-women's group.

My refusal was adamant. "Seriously, I don't want to go."

"There are good people at this one. Just try it out," she insisted.

So, I went. As myself. I didn't go to impress. I went to make new connections. I arrived at the venue, walked into the room, and sat down next to a woman with a simple brown bob, a sharp-looking suit, a fabulous statement necklace, and a hint of mischief in her eyes.

I flashed her a smile. "Hi."

She looked me up and down. "Meow."

*Did she just* meow *at me? What did that even mean? Was she hitting on me? What kind of networking group was this? I'd only been gone from Fargo for a year, was this the new greeting here? Was I to meow back at her? Or moo? Should I bark?*

What I said was, "I'm sorry?"

"I noticed your kitten heels when you walked in. They're really cute. Meow."

She was wicked funny! I burst out laughing and thought, *this woman is going to be my best friend.*

At some point later in the meeting, Shara related how she'd just completed a program with Dakota School of Banking, making her "The Bestest Banker That's Ever Banked."

*This gal gets better and better,* I thought.

Later that night, I ran into Shara again at an event hosted by the Fargo Chamber of Commerce, where I overheard her telling someone else about her recent certification. When I heard her say, "The Bestest Banker That's Ever Banked" to the gentleman she was standing with, I stepped in and said, "I apologize for the interruption, but you seriously need a new catchphrase."

Shara chuckled. It was settled. We would spend as much time together as humanly possible.

I was so thankful she brought her weird, quirky and snarky little self to the meeting that day. She had me at *meow.* Not only did she become one of my dearest friends, earning the title BFF Shara, she became a Nestie.

## Defining Me

With the return to my former employer, I quickly found myself longing for how it used to be. I was now at a new branch and, although I learned to love the people there, I never felt the same about the work itself. I didn't feel like me anymore. I knew I needed a change.

To figure out my life's purpose, I attended a Mastermind group that focused on the book *Think and Grow Rich* by Napoleon Hill. Shara tagged along. Initially, the whole book seemed coo-coo-cachoo. I didn't get it. It centered on "manifesting" stuff. Being a God-fearing woman, I almost felt the book left little room for a Supreme Being because it suggested I could think amazing things into reality with or without Him. On the other hand, the discussions we held around the topic of pursuing passion piqued my interest. The trouble was, I couldn't articulate what I was passionate about.

"I've never given serious thought to what I want to do," I admitted to the group in one session. "I got my degree, took the first job I was offered, and then kept going. It's as if I ended up on someone else's track but, because I'm good at it, I can't find my way off."

I wanted to share these thoughts with Jeremiah, but how do you explain that you're not sure you want to continue doing something that pays well and that you're good at just because you didn't think you were *passionate* about it? It didn't make sense. Not even to me.

The constant tugging at my heart felt a lot like discontentment. And discontentment felt like ingratitude.

*I should count my blessings,* I'd think. *There are people who can't find good work. Who I am to think this isn't good enough for me? What would Mom and Dad think? What would Grandma and Grandpa Seefeldt think? I shouldn't complain. It's unbecoming.*

I really started to struggle. I knew I didn't want to be in banking forever, but it felt wrong to want to leave my perfectly good job. I'd always found my value in my work. For the first time, I questioned if that was actually true. My restless heart was sleeping alone. Every. Single. Night. While I was out networking and meeting new people, I'd often feel isolated in a room full of strangers. People knew me as a banker, but that's not *who* I was, it's *what* I did.

Standing at a Business After Hours event hosted by the Chamber, I looked around the room. *Of all the people here who claim to know me, how many really know me? Would they be there for me if Jeremiah were suddenly struck with cancer? Would they bring me a casserole? Do they know my husband's name? Do they even know I have a husband?*

When I explained this to my Mastermind group, they suggested I think back to when I felt the most "me." That was easy. I felt the most me when I connected with an audience, when I used laughter, when I was teaching or training, and when I was challenging people to make changes in their lives. Did those moments hold value? Were they untapped talents? What could I possibly do to bring those things together? Most importantly, could I build a career around them?

## Bold Moves and Big Hair

The plan struck while I was sitting in a six-hour sales class offered by Dale Carnegie Training, with the incomparable Tamara Andersen as instructor. Tall, articulate, and engaging, she made the class fun and inspiring. Laughter, an audience, training. *Maybe this is something I could do,* I mused.

After doing some research, I decided to contact Tonya Stende, the owner of the franchise.

The phone call went something like: "Hi, Tonya. My name is Rebecca Undem and I've attended several programs that you've offered. I have an interest in doing the type of work you provide through Dale Carnegie. I'd love to visit with you if you are open to sharing how that might look."

I didn't realize that Tonya received calls like this regularly because the job seemed so cool and a lot of people thought they wanted to do it. She had many coffee meetings with people like the one she had with me. Not all of them turned out like mine.

As I made my way across Starbucks to the table, I was struck by Tonya's sincere, vibrant smile and—honestly—her big hair. I loved big hair. I feel about people who shy away from big hair the same way I feel about people who actually enjoy Three Musketeers bars: they're not to be fully trusted.

After approximately two minutes of small talk, I knew Tonya and I would be friends. One bold and somewhat-out-of-character call was all it took to change the course of my life.

I participated in my first full Dale Carnegie course in February of the following year, and there were times during the high intensity, dramatic sessions where I thought, *okay, nope. Maybe I was wrong. I can't imagine myself doing that in front of people. Maybe this isn't for me.*

The former drama queen was afraid of being too dramatic in front of people. Go figure.

When I shared my concerns with Tonya, she confided, "I remember having those same feelings. But once I got into the process of training certification, it didn't seem so scary."

With the completion of the twelve-week program in May, I eagerly anticipated the next steps, knowing that they would become clearer in June.

## Five Hundred Miles

Around this time, Mom called to ask if I could accompany her on her first buying trip for a new business she was starting in September.

In 1996, Grandpa and Grandma Seefeldt retired from Ben Franklin. The store had new owners who eventually opened another business right next door that provided custom framing services and floral design. My mom was the floral designer. This change probably came at the perfect time because crafting was becoming a thing of the past, and Mom had developed a true love and talent for fresh floral design. But now she had a plan: she was opening a pumpkin patch on the farm.

With her love of gardening and flowers and Dad's history of farming, Mom wanted to offer an experience where people could taste a slice of country living. A couple from our community had just retired from the only pumpkin patch in town, so the timing was perfect.

Two new buildings were being constructed on the farm, a retail shop and a large hoop barn. The retail shop was all hers, a place she could combine all of her talents. I was delighted to be asked to help with the buying trip, a nine-hour drive to a cash-and-carry market in Madison, Wisconsin. The two of us would find merchandise to fill her store.

One early June morning, I drove south forty-five miles to Wahpeton, where I'd park my car to join Mom for the rest of the journey. I hopped into the passenger seat, bursting with curiosity.

"So, what's going on with this business of yours?" I was tense with excitement.

"Oh, honey," she started, "I'm so excited about this business! But I worry that the shop won't be ready in time. The hoop barn is all done except for the floor. I think Tom has that figured out, but you know how he can be." She glanced at me. "The pumpkins are all planted and they're growing up quickly. Around the Fourth of July, we'll need help with weeding the patch. Do you think you guys could come back and help?"

"Sure. What are you doing for advertising and marketing?"

"I can't even think that far ahead with all the construction going on. I feel like I'll need every last minute just to get the farm ready for this." A worried frown creased her forehead. "I was hoping to have a website and write a blog, but you know me and computers." She heaved a sigh. "So that might just be a dream that won't happen this year."

As I listened to Mom talk, I knew she had bitten off more than she could chew. I changed the subject to the purchases we would make at market.

After getting settled into the Sheraton in Madison, I confided my dream of working for Dale Carnegie. She knew my frustration with banking since we'd returned to Fargo and was happy to learn I was exploring other avenues.

"Sometimes, I just wish I could come home and work with you," I admitted with a wistful sigh.

"Well, maybe you will!" Neither of us actually believed that could happen.

The next day, we arrived at the market and realized we should have come much sooner. It was like Black Friday at Best Buy. The line into the main arena of the convention center was already so long that the end of it trailed outside. When the doors opened, the crowd surged forward. We were focused and sharp, prepared to make quick decisions about what we'd buy. If we liked it and we had room for it, we bought it. *We handled it.*

Throughout the long grueling day, we made copious mental notes that eventually transferred to physical notes about what we'd do differently in the future. Enjoying a post-market-frenzy beverage, I commented, "Seriously, Mom, I have the best time with you. Today was so much fun. Tiring and overwhelming, but fun."

"I can't imagine doing this with anyone else either," she said.

I was looking for a change, although this wasn't exactly what I had had in mind. Was I losing it? What was I thinking?

"Do you think it would work for me to move back and help you?" I said, surprised to hear myself say the words.

"Are you serious? I would absolutely *love* that. Your dad and I have had a few conversations about him slowing down eventually. Between the seed business and farm, he could use more help. Do you think Jeremiah would ever want to consider buying in and maybe one day taking over Dad's ownership?"

I took a long swig of my beer, contemplating the idea.

Jeremiah had returned to Oakes the past several years to help with harvest . He wasn't thrilled with his current job, but his work day was 8-5, allowing him to be on the golf course every evening while I networked or met with friends. Would he want to give that up to become a farmer?

*Jeremiah will think I'm nuts! Could we really do this? Why do I feel excited just thinking about it?*

"Gosh, Mom, I don't know." I wasn't sure how much to reveal. "I just can't see him being on board with this. There's no way your business could financially sustain me. Although, *maybe*," I stressed the word, uneasy about committing my new friend, "Tonya would agree to me working from Oakes." Another concern popped into my mind and out my mouth. "We just purchased our house and I know the market is softening in the area. I honestly can't imagine Jeremiah and I both quitting our jobs and becoming self-employed. It seems crazy!"

"Well, your dad and I are now self-employed, too. We can all be crazy together!"

The buying trip seeded a string of conversations about us moving back. All I really knew was that Mom needed me. She needed more help getting the farm ready in time to open on September 12. I really wanted to do this for her.

As I made my solo journey the forty-five miles back to Fargo, I started to second-guess everything we'd discussed on our 500-mile road trip. When Mom and I were together, I focused on all the exciting aspects of this proposal; alone, I fixated on everything that could go wrong. For crying out loud, I didn't even know what I'd be doing for work. How would we live? Where would we live? What were we thinking? Smart girls had a better plan than this.

When I pulled into our driveway that evening, I was almost afraid to tell Jeremiah what Mom and I had hatched.

"Hey, how was the trip?" he asked.

"Good. It was good. Uh, want to hear my idea?" I couldn't muster much enthusiasm.

For some reason that I still don't fully understand, Jeremiah listened to my proposal. He actually said he'd consider it. I never expected that.

"Well, it seems like you and your mother have everything figured out. Has anyone even talked to Tom about this yet?"

He was right. Like good wives do, we had figured it out. We planned out what this new venture should look like for them without even consulting them. More, ahem, gentle nudging.

When we did actually consult Dad, he said in his typical, laid-back farmer way, "Well, it's not like we don't have enough work to do."

True enough, Dad. True enough.

## Getting My Ducks in a Row

While Jeremiah gave my half-baked idea some thought, I visited with Tonya about how the Dale Carnegie partnership would function if I moved. Could I work from Oakes? Clearly it would be different, but could it be done? If I was willing to work on 100% commission as a sales person and support their existing business as an adjunct facilitator, it could. Yikes. Talk about scary. A 100% commission? That was a far cry from the Estee Lauder counter!

I phoned my Nesties. I needed counsel and I needed to run this harebrained idea by friends who would be truthful, blunt even. I was looking for a swift kick in the rear, someone to say, "What? That's ridiculous! You'll never be happy in a small town!"

Over coffee, I shared my idea with Shara.

"Of course you'll do this," she said.

I searched her face for snark and sass but saw none. "You're … serious?"

"Rebecca, you love your family. You clearly love the farm. You already know you can work with your mom. I think because you have the Dale Carnegie thing besides, this is just the fresh start you need. Jeremiah will do great being self-employed."

Shara was on board.

Missy was less cheerleader-like but thought the plan made perfect sense and loved the idea of the pumpkin patch. I could sense a bit of envy in her voice. As a new mommy, she would have given anything to be closer to her parents. She was excited about opportunities to see me in Oakes when she came back to visit them.

Missy was on board.

I was most nervous about telling Koree because I already felt like a scared little girl compared to her wild and adventurous life in the military. I couldn't even make it living one state away from my family and now I hoped to move back to my little town. Would she see me as a loser? If she did, she never voiced it. In typical Koree fashion, she didn't dispense advice, she asked good questions and supported my plan.

Koree was on board.

I had the support of my Nesties. If this whole thing turned out to be a disaster, at least I had a team to help me through it.

Equipped with information about options for my employment, Jeremiah and I went back to Oakes for the Fourth of July weekend and helped my parents weed Mom's new pumpkin patch. As we sweated through our clothing from the physical labor, we passed time by singing songs and cracking jokes. Dad smiled and shook his head as I quipped, "If this was always your plan, you two should have considered having more kids!"

We did what we could to push along the progress of the new buildings and talked to my parents in concrete terms about this move. I had never, *never* planned return to Oakes. Needless to say, I was freaked out.

When we returned to Fargo, I had a final issue to clear up. "If we do this and it doesn't work out, are you going to say I pushed you into this?" I asked bluntly.

"No," said Jeremiah. "I do think you're pushing hard for this, but we are making the decision together and I won't hold anything against you. Are you sure this is *really* what you want?"

As I considered his question, my heart filled with doubt. I wasn't sure. I wasn't sure I could live again in my small town. I wasn't sure how I'd handle being a farmer's wife. After all, *this wasn't my plan.*

My screaming doubts were silenced by the reminder that my parents truly needed us. Way back when, my grandparents moved to Oakes because of a family business. My parents had remained in Oakes to support a family business. Now, I liked the idea of being involved in our family's business—an opportunity to carry on a legacy. And, although I never uttered it aloud, I knew Jeremiah was up to the task.

"I am not one-hundred-percent sure, but I think this is a chance we need to take," I admit.

We put our house on the market. Jeremiah was back in Oakes for good by the middle of July. From idea to formation to execution, this plan had taken a whopping five weeks. Whew.

A lot of people thought we rushed the process. Well, we did. We had to. Mom needed help immediately and Jeremiah went back to Oakes to help with construction and dirt-moving, the manly stuff that needed doing to get the farm ready for opening. I stayed behind to wrap things up and get the house sale moving along. I was able to stay on longer than two weeks at the bank because I wasn't going to a competitor. My plan was to move to Oakes on August 8. We'd be living with Mom and Dad—but just until the house sold. Then we'd start a new life. Just Jeremiah, me, and our little dog Tyke, who we had adopted into our family a year earlier.

At least, that was my plan.

# Rogue Duck

One early August morning, as I was getting ready for work, it occurred to me that my period was late. I brushed the thought aside until I was driving to the bank and realized it was actually more than a week late. I swung into a gas station to purchase a pregnancy test but waited until I got home that evening to follow the simple instructions: pee on the stick and wait.

As I waited, a million thoughts ran through my mind. The timing couldn't be worse. In three days, I wouldn't have a regular paycheck. What about health insurance? We were selling our house …. I was a planner. I made plans. My plans were good. I did *not* plan this.

The timer beeped on my phone. The three minutes were up.

I slowly walked to the bathroom and peeked over the top of the counter at the magic stick of altered destinies. I picked it up for a better look. I couldn't interpret it. I snatched the box out of the garbage, shuffled through the French and the Spanish, and found the instructions, but I was still puzzled. None of the example windows showed exactly what I observed in the one in my hand. *What?*

The next morning after a networking meeting, I pulled Shara aside. "So, I took a pregnancy test last night."

She anxiously nodded. *"And?"*

"Well, the results were inconclusive."

She snorted, "What do you mean, 'inconclusive'?"

"Well, one line means I'm not pregnant and two lines means I am and I saw … one-and-a-half lines."

She cocked an eyebrow. "What do you mean, *one-and-a-half* lines?"

Feeling more than a little defensive, I wished I had just brought the stupid test along. "Well, there were two pink lines, but one was fuchsia, and the other was so faint and so pale, that it was more like a half of a line."

She nearly choked on the Frappuccino she was swigging. As she wiped the whipped cream from her upper lip, she looked me right in the face and said, in her tough love voice, "Friend, you're pregnant. A faint line is a line. If there were two lines, you're pregnant."

"No. I can't be. Didn't you hear my explanation of the lines?"

"Yes, I did. But, a line's a line. You're pregnant. You better go pick up a digital test because you can't talk yourself out of those results. It will literally say Pregnant or Not Pregnant."

I freaked out right there on the street. I hugged her. I started to cry. I jumped up and down a little. I felt like a crazy person. She laughed at me, the way only a BFF is allowed to, gave me a big supportive hug, and left. On my way back to my office, I swung into a CVS and picked up not one but two packs of digital pregnancy tests. I wanted to be one-hundred-percent certain, and I figured if one was good, two must be better. I would double-check my work.

I ran straight to our office bathroom and waited those same three excruciating minutes.

So it was there, in the bathroom of the bank lobby that would be my workplace for another two days, I discovered I was pregnant with our first child. I picked up the stick and shook it as if it were a Magic 8 ball and I could get it to change its mind. Nope, the writing was on the wall. I was pregnant.

Assaulted by a wide range of emotions, I looked at my face in the mirror and judged my reflection. My expression went from thrilled to terrified. Tickled to tormented. Flabbergasted to fearful.

In addition to our enormous lifestyle change, we were adding a baby. I felt like I was having an out-of-body experience. We were moving back to Oakes. We wouldn't have a steady income. We had a house to sell, so we'd be *living with my parents*. We had no employer-paid health insurance. How was *that* for a plan? Who got pregnant at a time like that? Well, apparently, me.

For five years of marriage, Jeremiah and I had been fielding the question, "When are you guys going to have kids?" Children were always part of my plan, but I didn't sit around as a young girl dreaming of becoming a mom. My dreams involved business suits, big promotions, and over-priced coffee. I had never felt the need to please anyone by having children, not even Mom or Grandma Seefeldt, who adored babies as much as anyone I'd ever met.

Jeremiah and I were accustomed to taking loads of flack for it. At Grandpa and Grandma Seefeldt's house one Christmas, Sara and Sadie and I asked how they knew it was the right time to have kids.

Grandpa, in his gruff, no-nonsense way responded, "Well, we didn't sit around talking about it, that's for sure."

I felt like that was a direct shot at me, as Sara already had Tyler and Sadie wasn't yet married. Still, I preferred talking about it before doing something so final. So permanent. The finality of having kids freaked me out the most. I liked having the freedom to change my mind. Once you've had them, you don't get to change your mind about kids.

There was no turning back now. How on earth was I going to tell Jeremiah?

It was one thing for him to be open to this enormous life change we'd already chosen, but now to tell him this, too? I couldn't even fathom it.

I only had two days to plan the perfect way to tell him. Should I take him out for a candlelight dinner? It was a nice idea in theory, but we would be in Oakes—where you couldn't light a candle in public without everyone wondering about what you were celebrating. I could just imagine: *What's going on with them? Have you heard anything special about the Undems?*

The Mayberry rumor mill would start churning before we could leave the restaurant.

Yep, the candlelight dinner was out.

What about an elaborate reveal involving the whole family? Jeremiah was *super* private. He'd *hate* that. So, instead I decided to get him the perfect gift. Why not give him the original messenger?

I wrapped up the magic stick of altered destinies. I bought him a book about being a daddy. I painstakingly selected the *perfect* wrapping. I added the *perfect* bow. I chose the *perfect* location: the most romantic place in my parents' house, my childhood bedroom. Think of the magic.

I took him by the hand, walked up the stairs to my bedroom, handed him the perfectly wrapped package, and said, "Well, here's to our new adventure."

"Awe, you bought me a gift."

I muttered, "I kinda felt like I had to."

He opened it, and missing the book entirely, stared at the bottom of the stick because it was flipped over in the packaging. In a totally man-like way, he said, "I don't get it. What is this? A highlighter?"

I just sighed. "Yes. It's a highlighter with a specially *highlighted* message for us. Why don't you turn it over?"

He did. When he looked back up with me, with the most emotion I swear I'd ever seen him muster, he said, *"Really?"*

I broke down and wailed, "You're excited? You're really okay with this? Are we going to be okay? I can't believe this is happening right now!"

I completely lost my shit.

My husband stepped forward and put his arms around me. "Yes, I'm excited. You're okay. We're okay. This is going to be okay. Actually, it's going to be awesome."

I was so thankful for his poise, concern, and care for me and my fragile state of mind. I needed him more in that moment than I ever had before. Thankfully, he was thrilled. My family? They were thrilled. But, as thrilled as I was, all I saw was the big headline:BROKE, HOMELESS, PREGNANT. It was a bad reality TV series. *My* bad reality TV series.

# Oakes, North Dakota

Moving back to Oakes was a lot more than I bargained for emotionally. In my head, I was thinking it would be like a never-ending Easter weekend that felt more like a mini-reunion. I wasn't prepared for how I'd feel when I came back to be one of them.

I hated the feeling that I might be judged based on who I used to be—younger, more naïve, smart-mouthed and skinnier, which was more than slightly annoying. Would everyone still think of me as a drama queen? *I'm a grown woman,* I reminded myself. *I'm a grown woman.*

I didn't care about hunting, couldn't pull off camouflage clothing, and no longer played softball. When people asked me what I did for fun in Oakes, I had no viable answer. I felt misunderstood and lonely. Because I liked shopping, makeup, and clothes, I felt I ran the risk of being labeled High Maintenance.

Then there was the enormous change in our family dynamic. I hadn't expected the nature of our relationship with my parents to change as much as it did. Jeremiah and I had lived independently for five years as a married couple. In that time, through moves and jobs, we'd always enjoyed visiting my parents on weekends or when they'd make a trip to see us. We played cards, we drank beer, and we laughed hard, staying up too late most of the time. It was precious time designated to enjoy each other's company.

By moving back, I traded those memorable moments for daily interaction. I traded our joy and excitement for the mundane and routine. We didn't sit around having fun. We had work to do. Hard work. My parents didn't embrace shortcuts at all.

According to Jeremiah, the most difficult thing about working with my dad every day was that exact issue: my dad did *everything* the hard way. In addition, he was too stubborn to slow down and discuss what might be a better option. He was hard-charging and independent. His way was the right way.

Dad knew it, too. "I'm like a bull in a china shop," he admitted. "When I see something I want done, I charge in and make it happen, even if it's not always the best way."

Even though he and Jeremiah were now business partners, Dad often charged ahead without regarding Jeremiah's thoughts and opinions, leaving him feeling less like a partner and more like a hired man. When my husband discussed his concerns, I struggled with my responses. As one half of Team Undem, my allegiance was to Jeremiah. But I never anticipated how hard it would be to balance that with my role of daughter.

Then there was the sheer inconvenience of it all.

Never exactly a travel destination, North Dakota was mostly rural with ninety percent of the land dedicated to farms and ranches. Now, here we were in Oakes, a mere speck in the southeast corner of the state map. Not that I was complaining. We weren't totally isolated. Fargo was only 110 miles northeast. And Minneapolis was just four-and-a-half hours away. Why, it was only a hop, skip and a jump to … nowhere.

With a population of just over 1,800 people, Oakes boasted nine churches, four bars, three gas stations, one grocery store, and almost no available housing—which comically aligned with our overall priorities: God, beer, fuel, food and, lastly, shelter.

Thank goodness for Aberdeen, South Dakota, which offered the nearest Target. So what if it was in another state and roughly 71.2 miles south? The Starbucks there made it worth the drive. Honestly.

I *loved* coffee. I didn't necessarily consider it an addiction. More of a ... passion. I was passionate about having coffee when I wanted it. *Right* when I wanted it. Fortunately, Oakes had its own amazing little coffee shop, Sweets 'n Stories, where the owner Heather made a simply incredible macadamia nut Breve (with two shots of espresso and a half pump of syrup).

But, say, I happened to wake up early. I couldn't expect Heather to get me a cup of coffee at 6 a.m. Because she wouldn't. She wasn't open that early. So my only options were the gas station—or my Keurig. Problem was, I needed a cup of coffee so I could function enough to make a cup of coffee. That was the wrong that only Starbucks could make right. I wanted someone to hand me a mug of java, perfect and already made.

I was totally unprepared for the random hours that business owners kept. This was a major pain in the butt to contend with, initially. I was still in big-city mode so I naturally planned a route for errands, efficiently mapping out where I was going and in what order. There were times when I glanced at the clock while running errands and I thought, *Hey! I have a package to mail. I'll swing by and take care of this now.* I swung into the post office, pulled on the door, but found it locked. It was 10:05 a.m. and the place was closed.

I didn't know why—or if or when they would re-open. It was as if hours of operation ended in "-ish."

I was pregnant, cranky, and hormonal. I just wanted *what* I wanted *when* I wanted it. Those adjustments were challenging. But I only had to contend with those frustrations when I left the farm and, initially, I rarely left the farm.

## Potters Way

We had exactly six weeks until Mom's opening weekend for the pumpkin patch, and we had ten weeks' worth of work yet to do. From sunup to sundown, Mom and I worked through the items on her to-do list. Dad and Jeremiah worked through Dad's list.

The shop was only about fifty percent complete. We had all the displays to build for the grounds and in the corn maze, Mom needed to merchandise the shop after it was completed, and we still needed to pick all the produce and fill the barn with it.

Despite the Herculean tasks facing me, I was outside every single day and simply loved being in nature and working with my mom. I stood on the porch of our shop one day, deliriously satisfied. "I hope we can figure out a way for me to not work for anyone else and just work together on the farm."

We were surrounded by people who were delighted to have us back. One afternoon, Grandpa Karas stopped by the farm to check on our progress. He watched as we mounted the new shop sign: Potters Way. Mom had named her business after Isaiah 64:8: "We are the clay, You are the potter. We are all the work of Your hand."

Grandpa, who had become even more of a softie in his older age, put his arm around me. Together we read the signage. "It's nice to have you back here." He squeezed me to him, a bit of moisture dampening his eyes.

Thankfully, the good Lord smiled down on my pregnancy, because I really didn't have time for morning sickness. Being pregnant for the first time was awesome. Since we were living with them, Mom was able to pamper me. She cooked for me, made my snacks, and let me rest when I needed it. It was a pregnant woman's Eden.

Oddly, I didn't fret about our uncertain future. I fully believed a mother's presence provided that much comfort. My former life was a blurry recollection like you experience waking up from a dream, unable to tell if it really happened or not. My new life was an alternate universe. It was a good thing we had so much work to do; it kept me preoccupied with little time to consider how much my life had changed.

My role at Potters Way included helping Mom with advertising, marketing, and updating the website and blog. I also served as bookkeeper, taking that unexciting task off Mom's plate.

As the grand opening day approached, Mom was a nervous wreck. The fear that no one would come haunted her. My parents had made a significant investment in their property to bring this dream to life. It was an enormous gamble.

A gamble that paid off.

Thousands visited our farm on opening weekend. The response was overwhelming. Shara and her family made the 110-mile drive to show their support by being our first customers. Many families returned more than once during the season. We couldn't know that we offered what would become an annual family tradition for many in our area.

Mom wanted to offer a little slice of country living. Apparently, people wanted the whole pie!

The entire family was involved in Mom's new business adventure. Frailer now, Grandma Rodine spent one whole weekend as our official hostess. She coined her own greeting: "Welcome to Potters Way. Come in, look around, and spend the day." Her sweet, lilting voice and warm smile was an invitation in itself.

Grandma Seefeldt washed all the windows the week before we opened and made pumpkin pies from scratch on Sundays. Even extended family members helped. Karen and her family, Dan and his family, and Sara and her family (Tyler now had a little sister, Ellie) pitched in.

After a wildly successful Saturday, everyone on Mom's side of the family gathered at the shop for dinner. Asking us to join her in a toast, Mom raised a glass and blubbered a bit. "To my family. I could never have done this without you. We are so thankful you're all here, and we're so excited to share with you that … we're going to be grandparents!"

The room erupted with tears and laughter. No one voiced worries about our future. No one fretted about how Jeremiah and I would make it work. Our family was expanding, and that was worth celebrating.

## Being Evasive

At times during our first few months in Oakes, I'd travel to Fargo to meet with Tonya and Tamara or help out with a training. Inevitably, I'd run into someone I knew. When we had decided to leave Fargo, I only shared the news with my Nesties, my employer, and the Dale Carnegie women.

Naturally, when I visited, people would say, "Rebecca! Wow! I haven't seen you in so long! How's the bank?"

I would return their greetings and say, "Oh, I, uh, left the bank in August."

"What? I hadn't heard that! Where are you now? Do you have a business card on you?" Most assumed I'd accepted a job with a competitor.

Each time this happened, I was overcome by embarrassment, too uncomfortable to explain the choice we'd made. I felt ashamed. Hoping they'd move on from the topic, I'd quietly mumble, "Oh, uh, we moved back to Oakes."

Once I'd said that loud enough to be heard, I always anticipated *the look*. The look that suggested they were thinking, *Really? Why would you do that? And here I thought you were a real go-getter. Did your dreams die? What happened to you?*

When faced with someone from my professional past, I felt like I had squandered my potential by moving home. Like I was some sad, unfulfilled version of the woman I was supposed to become. It was hard not to question whether I'd ever feel professionally fulfilled in Oakes.

Each trip to Fargo was a painful reminder of all I'd left behind. I loved the hustle of the city. I loved meeting people for coffee dates and happy hour cocktails. I loved shopping for shoes and clothes and trying new restaurants. It was thrilling. It was exhilarating.

Now life was simple. Quiet. Boring, even.

I could hide from these feelings when I was on the farm. I felt like *me* when I was digging in the dirt with my mom and working on her business.

Our fall pumpkin patch season had lasted four weekends.

Immediately after, we offered a Haunted Farm for Halloween. On Black Friday, we reopened for a four-weekend Christmas season that lasted right up until Christmas Eve.

"I don't know how I'd have made it through if you hadn't moved back to help," Mom admitted as we sat down for Christmas dinner.

Her admission made my heart smile. As we bowed our heads for prayer, I considered how amazing God's timing is. Even though my unplanned pregnancy seemed horrendous at the time, if I had discovered I was pregnant any sooner, we never would have moved back to Oakes. Despite my inner struggles, I was thankful we were there.

## The Great Shakedown

When winter set in and Mom's business slowed to a halt, I had too much time on my hands. As I approached the end of my pregnancy, my perfectionism reared its ugly head and things got sketchy. Anxious because we still hadn't sold our home in Fargo, I felt we were wearing out our welcome in my parents' home. Besides, I was *never* alone. Everyone needs their space and we didn't have any.

In February, we purchased a house in Oakes after deciding to rent out our home in Fargo on a two-year contract. Because of our recent status as self-employed, we didn't qualify for typical financing. Unlike Dad years earlier, we chose to ask for help instead of living in a cardboard box. He pledged his land as collateral so we could secure the funding for our house. What a blow. A mere six months earlier, I was helping others secure home financing and here I was, not in a position to buy my own.

The house needed a little love, so we tore into it immediately and completed the projects about a week before my due date.

I felt awesome. I had successfully carried the baby to term. I lived in my own home. I was cooking our meals. I was ready to be a mom and start rocking small town life.

On April 7, 2009, at 5:55 a.m., Andrew Thomas Undem arrived.

I always considered myself a strong woman. I knew what needed to be done and I did it, rarely complaining. I was consistent about wearing big girl panties. I had read all the childbirth books. I even planned my birth experience and got pretty much exactly what I wanted: in Oakes, with Dr. Rup, one of our long-term doctors. Throughout my prenatal visits, I insisted on delivery without drugs.

I was fully prepared.

Jeremiah and I took Lamaze classes from a couple in our community, who until this interaction, I had only ever known as "Hannah's parents." Hannah was a classmate. During my childhood, most of my family's friendships formed through church. Hannah's family was Catholic; mine was Lutheran. We didn't run in the same circle.

Sharon had spent most of her professional career as a labor and delivery nurse and passionately guided us through the process of delivering a child naturally. Her husband, Tom, who was the business manager at our school, took an active role in leading the husbands through what they would experience as our "labor partners."

This was the first of many eye-opening experiences in which I got to know people in Oakes for who they really were instead of by some random, familial connection or other preconceptions that existed in my mind.

At every appointment, Dr. Rup cautioned, "You know, Rebecca, you don't have to be a hero. The pain will be very intense."

He might as well have said, "I double dog dare you to get through this without drugs!"

For a first delivery, it happened fast, under three hours from my water breaking to the baby arriving. I was blessed to work with an amazing nurse who told me several times she'd never seen a first-time mom handle herself like I did.

When I got a rush of adrenaline somewhere around eight centimeters of dilation, I proclaimed, "I feel like a superhero!"

She smiled. "Well, you kind of are."

Dr. Rup walked in as I was ready to push. I peered at him across my belly. "Dr. Rup! I did it! See? I *knew* I could do it!"

Despite his masked face, I could see the corners of his eyes crinkle, hinting at a grin.

I wasn't weak or pathetic. I was Rebecca Type-A Undem and when I wanted something to happen, I made it happen. I *handled* things. I did them *well*.

Nearly fifty visitors passed through my hospital room in the first twenty-four hours of Andrew's life. Mom and Dad arrived first, followed by Grandpa and Grandma Seefeldt. Shara drove two hours from Fargo. I was on top of the world.

Then, we came home.

Where I experienced a shakedown. By my own offspring. Those first few weeks home with Andrew were some of the darkest times in my life.

What on earth was the hospital thinking to put me in charge of an hours-old infant?

The nurse did not send me home with a confidence-building binder chock full of parenting instructions. There was no handbook. And the books I *had* read didn't detail a perfect plan for *my* child.

Here's the thing: with kids, you don't instinctively know what needs to be done. What if I ruined my baby?

Of course, even with a handbook, I would need updated versions at each major milestone. Puberty 2.0. First crush 3.2. My mid-20s daughter just came back home to live with us 4.1. We'd need to build a library. Or invest in additional digital storage.

But here's the other thing. Babies level the playing field. A tiny, wrinkled bundle of neediness doesn't give two craps about your background, your education, your current professional status, or—for crying out loud—your dreams for the future.

There were a few major factors contributing to my shakedown (outside of my unrealistic expectations that I could somehow *prepare* for being a mother). I was alone most of the time, so my days were long; Andrew was fussy and I really hated nursing.

My loneliness stemmed from three areas: My mother had been my roommate throughout my pregnancy and, suddenly, she wasn't there all the time. Jeremiah's first busy season of delivering and treating seed was upon us. Flooding in the Oakes area made farmers more anxious than usual, and the road that went out to our farm was covered in water, making the typical five-mile trip a forty-mile trek. Caught up in mothering, I wasn't really present for my husband's worries during that first year as a business owner. Much like my parents had in their early years, Jeremiah and I were fighting separate battles.

And, lastly, I hated how I turned inward, avoiding people. I was ashamed for feeling displeased about being a new mom—which overshadowed my extroversion. The only people I let into my self-focused world were Mom and Jeremiah. Jim and Teri wanted to come and visit within those first two weeks and I asked Jeremiah to tell them no. In true small-town fashion, casseroles appeared. Help was offered. But I turned away from family and friends during this difficult time of adjustment.

Andrew was a fussy little guy. He wasn't colicky, but he did his fair share of crying. His tummy was upset a lot, he struggled with pooping, and he kept me up at night. He spit up *constantly*. I was an anxious mess.

Then, there was the nursing.

Rebecca Type-A Undem didn't cut corners. She made informed choices. And nursing was one of those choices—the informed, healthiest, and right choice for my baby. Yeah, well, it proved not to be the right choice for *me*. Never in my life had I experienced so much guilt and anguish over something touted as the "best bonding experience" and "most natural thing" a mother would ever do.

I hated every. Single. Second. Of. It.

Each time Andrew cried, I thought, *Oh, no, you want to eat again. I'll change you, I'll burp you, I'll do anything, just please, please, don't be hungry.*

I had plenty of help. Lactation consultants arrived. They assured me I was doing a great job. If I was doing such a great job, why was I in pain all the time? Why did I hate it so much?

Mom came over after church on Good Friday, took one look at me and said, "Why didn't you tell me you were having such a hard time? Go to bed. I'll watch the baby." She turned to Jeremiah—who was content to have someone take charge—and ordered, "You're going to the bar with Tom. Leave this to me."

Gathering our sweet puppy, Tyke, into my arms, I stumbled back to my bedroom and laid down on the bed. Tyke looked at me with the sad eyes as if to ask, *What did you do to us, Mom?*

What *had* I done? I wasn't cut out to be a mom. I wasn't nurturing enough. Andrew deserved better than me. Maybe Mom should take him. She loved babies. *I don't think I'm supposed to be thinking about who might want my baby.*

What was wrong with me?

## Meet and Greets

Thankfully, we were surrounded by the original village that helped raise me.

Andrew was a little less than a month old and we took both Grandma Seefeldt and Grandma Rodine up to Fargo with us to attend a dual family baby shower hosted by Cousin Sara and my dad's sister, Sharon. These two families were double related; Sharon married my Grandma Seefeldt's nephew Mike, making their kids both my first and third cousins. (Their daughter, Jen, and I hashed it out when we were kids, deciding there was nothing illegal or immoral about it, much to our relief.)

At the shower, I got to introduce our little guy to a host of family members at one time. But I felt totally isolated when I hid in an upstairs bedroom to nurse Andrew while everyone else visited downstairs. Our method of "latching" did not warrant an audience; it was so acrobatic I struggled for modesty.

Around this same time, I developed a strange rash on my nipples, accompanied by searing pain. When thrush was diagnosed, I received a topical cream to treat it. After each application, my nipples needed to air-dry. To compound the inconvenience, it had to be washed off before each feeding. Instead of worrying about a tidy house when unexpected guests arrived, I had to remember to tuck away my nipples. Where was the dignity?

Even after the thrush cleared, pain was a constant companion.

Mom didn't get it. When she birthed us, most mothers formula-fed—because, you know, they didn't have Internet or Facebook to consistently shame them into compliance. Even so, she never dispensed advice on the subject. But she did push me to get out of the house.

"It's good for you and the baby," she urged.

One of our first house visits was to see Grandpa and Grandma Karas, who lived just across town. They looked upon little Andrew as if he were one of their own.

"You're Grandma's sweetheart," she cooed.

Grandpa smiled up at me with pride. "You did good, kid."

Andrew was nearly six weeks old when Koree and her husband, Jason, showed up in Oakes to visit. I wanted to pour my heart out to her, but with Jason there, I reserved my sad diatribe for a later phone call.

On Saturday, May 16, I awoke with the plan to spend the day with Mom at the farm. When I phoned, there was no answer. When I couldn't reach her, I finally called Dad on his cell.

"Grandpa Karas was airlifted to Fargo last night with what they think was a heart attack," he said. "I haven't heard anything yet. Jonda is at the hospital, so your mom is at their house watching the kids."

Grandpa had dealt with heart issues in the past, but I had just seen him and he appeared healthy. Worried, I got Andrew ready and drove to Jonda's. Mom answered the door. After scooting Jon and Jaci down the hall, she softly admitted, "He's gone, honey. Jonda just called. The kids don't know and she wants to tell them so I have to keep it together. Why don't you go home and I'll come over when she gets back."

Despite Grandpa's unexpected death, we found peace in the knowledge that he was in heaven having the most perfect meet-and-greet of all time with his first love—Jesus.

I left with a heavy heart. Our village wouldn't be the same without him.

## Surviving Rush Week

Grandma Seefeldt offered to watch Andrew so I could attend the funeral. I left her with bottles of milk I'd pumped. When I returned to pick him up, she said, "You know, Becca, I think Andrew's tummy troubles are because of your milk. Maybe your milk is bad. Maybe you should just try formula."

I nearly fell over.

*Give him formula! I couldn't just quit and give him formula. What if he contracted diphtheria or something worse? If I give him formula, he'd never get good enough grades to finish high school or get a girlfriend. Formula would ruin him.*

I left feeling worse than ever.

Seven weeks into my nursing distress, a lactation expert watched Andrew latch. As I caught my breath at the piercing pain, she commented, "The latch is perfect. You'll be pros in no time."

I should have shown her the door. When she declared with condescension, "All women can nurse. There's no reason why any woman can't"—my mother actually did.

When she closed the door behind the lady, Mom turned and said what had been on her mind since she first stormed the castle on Good Friday, "Honey, this is ridiculous. Since the beginning of time there have been women who couldn't nurse their children. That's why they had wet nurses. If you want to stop, you can. I hate seeing you like this. I doubt this is good for Andrew, either."

I couldn't help myself. I wailed in relief. Someone had given me permission to do what I wanted to do.

Later that evening, I hesitantly called Shara. Certain she'd breastfed her two children because, you know, she was so smart, I assumed she couldn't relate.

After listening to my woes, Shara shared her own struggles with nursing. "This is how I see it. Is boob juice laced with resentment and anger really better than formula offered with peace and contentment?"

I laughed out loud. She was the first person to acknowledge that there must be repercussions from anxiety-laden nursing. That phone call was just what I needed. I knew what I wanted to do. I wanted to quit. Sadly, as a first-time mom, I wasn't confident enough to give myself permission.

"You know, becoming a mother is nothing like I pictured," I confided to Shara. "I thought it would feel like I was joining a club, almost secretly hoping we'd meet occasionally, recite a pledge, and wear matching jackets with an emblem embroidered on the breast pocket." I paused and quipped, "Like FFA for moms!"

She laughed.

"But it's not a club." I tried to better express my thoughts. "It's more like a sorority where we get initiated during rush week with bizarre hazing and then constantly struggle with how much better all the other girls are at everything."

"Well," Shara retorted, "maybe we should start a club. The kind with matching jackets. We'll work on a secret handshake later!"

## Rural Living

Not long after I quit nursing, motherhood started to look a little better on me. When Andrew was four months old, I decided maybe I wasn't the worst mother on the planet. I could have normal conversations that didn't revolve solely around my nipples or my son's pooping schedule. The fog lifted and I started to enjoy being a mom.

Nothing changed me more than becoming a mother and I wasn't entirely sure I was pleased with the changes. I liked the woman I was B.C.—before childbirth.

Being at the mercy of an infant's whims was a difficult adjustment for a self-reliant and independent woman like me. The trial and error, the winging it, and the utter uncertainty of my efforts nearly overtook me.

When the old Rebecca began to emerge, all she wanted to do was go back to work. Work made sense and at work, she either succeeded or she failed. No uncertainty involved.

I had assumed that, once I became a mom, I'd feel differently about work. So many women had told me how everything changed when they shouldered motherhood; all they wanted was to be at home with their babies. I felt no such thing. I questioned why I didn't yearn to stay home with Andrew. No matter how hard I tried to picture myself as a stay-at-home mom, the result was like an unfocused snapshot. I couldn't see myself doing that.

I yearned for a sense of value and purpose, the same value and purpose I'd felt in my job. My work with Dale Carnegie had been curtailed due to pregnancy and Mom's business. I was anxious to get back into it.

I worked from home most days but had to travel for classes, opportunities which got me out of the house and out of Oakes and, frankly, kept me sane. The job was a natural fit and I was good at it, especially high-level conversations with business owners. And the position was practically ideal for my life: flexible enough to allow me to set my own hours, to support Mom's business, and to scale back during Jeremiah's busy times when he wasn't as available to help me.

Dale Carnegie allowed me to spend time with people who mattered most.

The initial Madison trip Mom and I had taken turned into an annual family affair. Dad, Jeremiah, and eight-week-old Andrew accompanied us. Although I no longer lived at the farm to help every minute, Mom's second season was successful. I was there as much as I could be.

On evening walks with Andrew and Tyke, when the vicious North Dakota mosquitoes were controlled enough to venture outdoors, I often took time to visit Grandma Seefeldt. No matter when we stopped by, whether she was working in the yard or ironing clothes in the kitchen, she would stop what she was doing and say, "Well, hi, Becky! Come on in!"

She offered me a beer and Andrew a snack, keeping her cabinet stocked with his favorite treats. While my other grandmas smoothed my worries with baked goods, Grandma Seefeldt soothed them with snacks and a drink. I watched Grandma open a can of Miller Lite and pour it into a glass and, even though she did nothing special to it, I always swore her beer tasted better. Just like her tea, which she served when it wasn't happy hour!

She and Grandpa became fond of Tyke, too, surprising because we never knew them to be animal people. When we'd leave for a weekend, they often dog-sat for us. In recent years, Grandpa had suffered several small strokes, leaving him with some cognitive damage—less talkative and occasionally confused. Little Tyke's companionship was therapeutic.

The summer after Andrew turned one, Mom and Dad asked Jeremiah and me to help landscape Grandpa and Grandma's yard. We pulled out all the existing rock and laid down barrier fabric, pulled out dying shrubs and planted new ones. With the four of us, the work was speedy but physical. I had mowed their lawn and shoveled their driveway a handful of times, but this was the first major project I'd helped them with. Grandma had a terrible time asking for assistance.

She made us lunch, fretting, "Oh, it's hot out there. Are you sure you're drinking enough water? I don't want you to wear yourselves out. Oh, it's too much work. You should quit. Really, just stop."

We forced, *er*, gently nudged her to sit in the house while we labored outdoors.

I was rocking small town life: I loved being a mom, I had developed great relationships with friends from church and (gasp!) friends from *other* churches, and I had a fantastic job that allowed me to put my family first. My position with Dale Carnegie provided for us more than adequately. I wouldn't have said that I needed more money to be happy. I was finally content.

## Back on the Ladder

Until one day, about two years later, when one of our clients offered me a position.

The HR director for a large, local nonprofit was in one of my training programs. At the end of the course, she approached me. "Rebecca, I have just put together a comprehensive workforce development plan. I'd like you to consider coming to work for us and managing the whole thing."

What? Work for them? I worked for me! I loved working for me. In fact, I was the best boss I'd ever had. (And the prettiest, the nicest, the smartest ....) But, because I tried to be open-minded to all opportunities that came my way, I responded, "Well, I'd be open to hearing more about it."

We had numerous coffee and lunch dates and, at some point in this discovery process, I learned the starting salary, which was barely less than Jeremiah and I had made *together* when we lived in Fargo. I couldn't help but dream of the clothes, shoes, and stuff I could buy with that kind of money.

The job would require me to travel to the main office in Jamestown two to three times a week. Otherwise, I could work from home. This was the perfect storm: I could raise my kids right there in Oakes, giving them that wide-open freedom of growing up that I had experienced, while holding an important position that made me feel valuable.

On paper, the job was perfect. Yet I struggled at the thought of working for someone else again. With Dale Carnegie, I had a ton of flexibility and my life was going great. I consulted My People.

Shara thought it was an incredible opportunity. "I've always wanted a seat at the table of a company. It sounds like your voice will be heard there."

My parents couldn't believe they were offering me that much money. "No smart person would walk away from that."

Koree's input? "With that kind of money, you can come visit me in California!"

Jeremiah was thrilled, of course. We had moved to Oakes at a time when farming was inherently less risky, with good commodity prices. His seed business was growing successfully. Despite the success, he often came home and shared the stress of his work. While many of our conversations revolved around his tricky relationship with my father, financial burdens were a regular part of our discussions. The security of this job would release a tremendous weight from his shoulders.

I scheduled a meeting with Tonya and Tamara. After I disclosed the details, they agreed it would be hard to make that kind of money in my current role. "We understand if you feel you need to accept." Disappointing them was hard, but I was grateful for their support.

Jeremiah and I had been rocking this self-employment thing for a while, and we really wanted to have another baby. This new financial security felt like a blessing from the good Lord above. The job I'd been waiting for. The career I'd dreamed of having. I was ready to hop back on the ladder and climb.

Prior to accepting the position, I visited the organization's headquarters where my boss explained the benefit package. Immediately, a slight tightening constricted my chest. I discounted it as nervous jitters. Then, she uttered a simple three-letter acronym: PTO. My chest contracted. I struggled to breathe. I hadn't had to ask anyone's permission to be gone for a day or to take a vacation in over two years.

*Really, is asking for time off that big of a deal? Remember, the salary? The huge salary? Do you know how many pairs of adorable shoes you'll be able to buy with this kind of money?*

Despite my doubts, I accepted the job, to start at the end of our third fall season at Potters Way.

## Leading Ladies

The sticky humidity of summertime subsided. The crisp autumn air was filled with the constant hum of combines in the fields and semis hauling grain. Grandma Rodine's health declined significantly.

Shortly after I graduated from high school, Grandpa and Grandma Rodine had moved off the farm into an apartment in town. When his Alzheimer's disease required more care than Grandma could provide, Grandpa had moved to the nursing home where Grandma visited him every single day until he passed away two years before we returned to Oakes.

To help keep her loneliness at bay, we visited Grandma at her apartment as much as we could, most often after church on Sundays. However, Grandma was famous for keeping her apartment at a "comfortable" 81 degrees, so we often dozed off, whereas Grandma kept an afghan on her lap to keep the chill away. Mom helped her with doctor's appointments and managed her medications. She loved Grandma Rodine as much as her own parents and was glad to serve her.

Eventually, Grandma needed more care and she, too, moved to the nursing home.

About a month into my new job, Mom and I had planned a trip to Minneapolis to do some Christmas purchasing for the shop. We stopped to see Grandma before we left, knowing she wasn't doing well. Dad and Aunt Sharon were with her. Aunt Pam and Aunt Kathy were on their way. Mom regretted leaving town, but knew Grandma would be surrounded by her children.

While we were checking into our hotel that afternoon, my cell phone rang.

"Mom's gone." Dad choked up. "She passed just a few minutes ago."

"Oh, Dad, I'm so sorry." Grandma Rodine hadn't been herself for a long time, so we were comforted, knowing she was with Grandpa again.

Mom cried with Dad on the phone and when she hung up, we hugged. "I feel bad that I wasn't there for your dad." But he had encouraged her to go, knowing the trip was necessary for her business.

At the prayer service, we mourned Grandma and learned to accept our family's new landscape. Out-of-town cousins recalled memories of their annual week-on-the-farm with Grandpa and Grandma. When Cousin Amy related her adventures, I suddenly realized I had never stayed with my grandparents for a long stretch of time. I didn't have memories with my grandparents that involved big moments; all of my memories were simple, mundane, uneventful. Grandpa and Grandma were part of my everyday life. I didn't have to wait for special trips; I could ride my bike down the road to see them.

I saw my childhood as if it were a quilt with large blocks. Instead of my grandparents being a prominent block, they were the thread running through the fabric of the whole piece.

A few weeks later, I turned thirty. Tamara, my former Dale Carnegie colleague, invited Mom, Andrew, and me to lunch at her house, about forty minutes outside of Fargo. We gladly made the drive because, when you're offered an opportunity to eat Tamara's food, you drive all night if you have to. While we were there, we toured some holiday open houses, planning to meet up with Shara in Fargo.

Romantic Jeremiah made an appearance, surprising me with a big bash in Fargo. A tough woman to surprise, I gave him lots of credit. The only downer was Grandma Seefeldt's absence. She wasn't feeling well and decided to stay home, highly uncharacteristic for her since she never missed an opportunity to spend time with family.

Mom and I stopped by her place the following evening to pick up Tyke. We knocked but didn't hear her typical, singsong, "Come on in!"

Letting ourselves in, we watched as she struggled to rise from her recliner. Obviously, she wasn't well. We were alarmed.

Mom pried a bit, but Grandma brushed her concerns aside. "Don't worry about me. I'm going to the doctor tomorrow to find out what's going on."

Later that that week, Jeremiah called me at work.

"What's up?"

"Beck, if you're able to, I think you should come home early," he began. "Your mom had to go into town to help Dorothy and she couldn't take Andrew with her."

"Is it really necessary for me to leave right now?"

"I don't really have any details but I think you should come home. Andrew's out at the farm with your dad."

The tone in his voice suggested I shouldn't argue. "Okay. I'll go straight there to get him. See you soon."

After I hung up, I briskly walked to my boss's office and told her I needed to go. The drive back to Oakes from Jamestown typically took me an hour and fifteen minutes. All the way home, I prayed to have no encounters with deer on my drive and that Grandma Seefeldt would be okay. I pulled into my parents' driveway exactly fifty-eight minutes after leaving my office.

When I walked into the house, I saw only my dad and I knew something was desperately wrong.

"What's going on?" I asked, hearing the urgency in my own voice.

"Honey, Dorothy was taken by ambulance to the hospital in Oakes today. Howard called your mom earlier and she went in to help him."

"She's in the Oakes hospital and was taken by ambulance?" I asked. "That seems weird. Is she okay? Where is Andrew?"

"Jeremiah took Andrew back home. Honey, it's not good. Karen and Dan are on their way here. It sounds like it was a major stroke."

Without another word, I got into my car and drove to the hospital. When I arrived, I was directed down a hall to the room right next to where I'd delivered Andrew. I slowly approached the open door and saw my family, along with Pastor O'Brien, gathered around Grandma. I caught Mom's eye. I searched her face for answers to questions I couldn't find the words to ask.

She only shook her head.

There was nothing to be done for Grandma. Mom gave the order to shut off the machines. The beeping faded and Grandma passed. The very heart of our family stopped beating for a moment.

I learned that Grandma had suffered a major stroke from an undetected brain bleed. After lunch that afternoon, she had sat down in her recliner for her daily power nap before her church meeting and she didn't wake up. When Grandpa couldn't rouse her, he called Mom, who called the ambulance.

Only seventy-six years old, Grandma Seefeldt was well known in our community. Since retirement, she had been a devoted volunteer for Meals on Wheels and at the Senior Center. She was still active in our church. She offered rides to people who needed them, checked up on people who had no one else, and even managed her friend's household when she left town to visit grandchildren.

Her death left a lot of people reeling.

Mom and her family managed to get through the funeral arrangements, the overwhelming outpouring of support—each requiring a handwritten thank-you, and the difficulty of dealing with the house and Grandpa's eventual transfer to the nursing home.

We all knew Grandma was strong but, as a family, we were shocked by how she had hidden Grandpa's degeneration. His cognitive state was much worse than anyone realized. The same held true for Uncle Gary, who lived in a group home in Valley City. Grandma made regular trips there to bring Gary home for major holidays. We simply had no idea how much effort it took because she didn't ask for help; it wasn't her way. She never complained because she loved them both and wanted to be with them. Family was everything.

The family put their grief on hold to make the necessary decisions. But, like lava boiling under the surface of the earth, the pressure built and sought release. When Mom was ready to talk about what she'd been through, I was there to listen, recognizing that she would never fully forget the images of that awful day when she got the call from Grandpa. While I tried to be the sounding board for her grief, two-year-old Andrew soothed her soul and grounded her in the moment, a welcome distraction from sadness.

I was riddled with regret over words not said and lessons not learned. Grandma knew so much she'd been willing to pass on. Yet, I hadn't mastered the art of canning. I never learned how to make lefse. I never learned how to quilt. Mostly, I wished I'd told her what she meant to me and to my family.

No one wanted to imagine life without Grandma Seefeldt. Our family had lost both our leading ladies. Now, although the plot would be different, the show had to go on.

The Christmas open house for Potters Way loomed on the horizon. Mom had to put her head down and plow through; it was too late to cancel. The shock of losing her mother was raw, but she had to open her shop and put on a smile.

Most difficult was the continual reminder that Grandma was gone. Every customer arrived bearing words of sympathy. Although gratifying, thoughtful, and kind, the steady stream of condolences was exhausting.

At the end of the season, Mom decided to stop offering Christmas at Potters Way. As the new matriarch of the family, she felt an overwhelming responsibility to somehow fill the big shoes Grandma left behind. She was determined to create the same sense of family that Grandma had at Christmastime. Mom brought Gary to stay with them at the farm.

On Christmas Eve, we did our best to maintain Grandma's rich traditions. We attended the 5 p.m. candlelight service. Mom prepared oyster stew, one of the Grandma's specialties. But Christmas was all wrong without Grandma's food, without her holiday cheer, without… her. I so desperately wanted to honor her memory. I felt like a failure.

I had a son and wanted to enjoy this Christmas with him. I needed my mom to help me create a warm, holiday spirit and she simply didn't have it to give. She was as disappointed as I was.

She was completely overwhelmed with the care of both Grandpa and Gary. After that night, she decided she'd never do Christmas Eve like this again with both Gary and Grandpa. No one could replace Grandma and she'd never enjoy the holiday with her grandchild if she kept trying.

A few days later, she shared a precious memory of the Christmas before.

With a major winter storm predicted, Jeremiah and I had left early to go to Jamestown for Christmas with his family. Mom phoned her folks. "With this storm rolling in, why don't you bring Gary and come out here and stay with us? It doesn't make sense for us to be here alone and you guys to be in town alone. We'll eat, play games, and watch Christmas movies."

"Oh, well, that sounds like fun!" Grandma said. Mom could hear Grandpa grumbling in the background, "No, we're not going to go out there."

Grandma gently nudged him and they loaded the car. It was the first time Mom's parents had ever stayed with them. Mom and Dad gave up their bedroom and slept upstairs in the guest bedroom.

The supposed blizzard was the real deal, snowing them in. Mom hustled and bustled in the kitchen while Grandma, Grandpa, Gary, and Dad played board games.

Grandma would say, "Oh, Jeanie, I feel bad that we're out here playing games while you're in the kitchen. Are you sure you don't want some help?"

"I'm good out here, Mom. I like listening to you guys playing games." Mom loved having them and thought Grandma enjoyed not bearing the full responsibility for Gary.

By the time she finished telling the story, tears coursed down our cheeks. "I'm so thankful for those precious days with my mom."

Grandma had allowed herself to be nurtured. That rarely happened. And Mom got to be the one to do it.

## Bright Spot

With the sudden loss of those two dear women in my life, I was thankful my new job to demanded my full attention. I threw myself into my work and, within the first six months, said to my boss, "I feel like we have enough work to last us at least twenty years." And I meant it. I believed I could grow within this position, staying there until retirement.

A big factor in taking the job was the security available to expand our family. About a year and a half later, we had our second son, Carter. A fully paid maternity leave was available, reaffirming my decision.

My due date was just a few days before opening day of the fall season at Potters Way, horrific timing. As babies do, Carter decided he was ready a little early and arrived three weeks ahead of schedule.

Because he was jaundiced, I decided to nurse to keep him healthy. But the day we came home from the hospital, I began pumping and bottle-feeding so I would know how much he was getting. When I was ready to quit pumping only after a few weeks, I had a moment of guilt. I called Shara.

"Tell me it's okay to quit. I'm just so busy trying to help Mom with her opening that I really don't feel like I have to time to devote to pumping."

"You know the answer to this but because I know you need to hear it, I'll say it. You can quit. You are not a sucky mom if you quit."

With her blessing, I quit. I didn't have the guilt or shame I'd experienced the first time around. Barring that one moment, I really didn't struggle with the decision at all. I had vowed I wouldn't let nursing rob me of the joy of those first few weeks like I experienced with Andrew.

On maternity leave, I was able to be out at the farm every single weekend to help Mom most of that season. The extended family got to meet Carter right away because we were all spending so much time together at Potters Way. Even the customers warmly welcomed our new addition. By this time, our community had become an extension of my family.

My entire experience with Carter as an infant was infinitely better than it was with Andrew. I was much calmer.

*I'm coming, baby*, I thought as I prepared his bottle during the middle of the night. As I rocked and fed him, I realized how much I treasured those moments. Maybe I was supposed to be a mother after all.

Something new stirred in me. My urge to return to work wasn't as clear as before.

The day I returned from my twelve-week maternity leave, I walked into the conference room expecting … what? Not an all-out party, but, well, maybe a little bit of confetti and some balloons? Defensive, I thought, *Really? No one even missed me? Doesn't my presence or at least my work add enough value that people notice when I'm gone?*

My bruised ego turned a little bluer when one of my colleagues approached me. "Oh, you're back. How was your vacation? And what did you have anyway?"

What the hell? Who called a maternity leave a vacation? What did I have? I had a baby.

Ready to get back into the swing of things, I had the standard issue mom-guilt of leaving my new baby in daycare. It was a tough first day.

But my colleague's comment prodded me to consider why I would trade time with my family to be with people that didn't know me or care enough to try. Once we entered the conference room, our CEO welcomed the new director in Fargo.

When Marilyn stood and introduced herself, she made great eye contact and exuded warmth. I liked her immediately. In fact, while I was leading the discussion on employee onboarding later that afternoon, I frequently caught her nodding in agreement. When she later shared her perspective, my thinking aligned with hers.

After the meeting, she initiated a conversation. "I love your perspective on what we discussed today. Would it be possible to have you come to our office and do some training for our staff?"

"I'd love to," I replied. "We'll have to work out the details."

Just as a sunny day offers hope and a welcome reprieve from consecutively gloomy February days in North Dakota, Marilyn was my bright spot in an otherwise tough day.

## Not So Super Super Bowl

A few months later, we had plans to hang out with some of our friends Super Bowl weekend. Carter, not quite five months old, had developed a bit of a cough and, as the week progressed, his condition worsened. He was sleepy, didn't want his bottles, and had a low-grade temperature.

On Super Bowl Sunday, I got up with him in the morning and knew something wasn't right. Worried, I told Jeremiah that I was taking him to the emergency room (the only option on a Sunday in Oakes) to have him checked out.

"Don't worry," I said. "I'll be back in time for our party."

After a five-hour wait and a battery of tests, I was stunned when the on-call doctor decided to admit Carter. They still hadn't determined what he had but they wanted to keep an eye on him.

Eventually, the attending physician came in and asked, "Has he looked like this all morning?"

Strung-out, hungry, and frightened, I frowned in my uncertainty. "Look like what?"

"His skin color. He's so dusky." She turned to the nurse. "What are his O-sat levels?"

The nurse shrugged. "We didn't take them."

The doctor raised her brows and the room suddenly hummed as nurses and technicians bustled around my baby. Tests showed his oxygen levels in the low 90s. A quick swab of his nose pointed to RSV, a serious upper respiratory virus that is common in babies and young children.

"We need to transport Carter to a higher care facility," the doctor said.

Shocked, I looked at her blankly and somehow managed to ask, "Transport him how?"

"We're already prepping the ambulance."

There was nothing super about that Super Bowl Sunday. I felt like I was coming unglued. I called Jeremiah with the news and gave him a short list of items to pack for me. Following their instructions, I climbed onto the stretcher and held Carter as they strapped me in and loaded us into the ambulance.

Curt, the paramedic who attended us, reassured me. "He is going to be fine. We just don't work with the really young ones very often and that's why we're going in the ambulance. If you can, try to keep him awake but also try not to let him cry. That's when his oxygen levels plummet."

How on earth was I supposed to keep Carter awake without him crying? He hadn't eaten all morning. *Lord, be with us.*

As the ambulance left the hospital garage, I felt vaguely comforted by the thought that my prayers would be supplemented by the prayers of the people we passed on our way. In small towns, people pray when they see an ambulance or a life-flight helicopter, certain that someone they personally know might be in trouble.

It was the longest two-hour ride of my entire life. I held my gray-skinned, limp, little one in my arms and prayed, *Lord, keep him calm. Help us get there safely.*

At the children's ICU, we were greeted by the doctor who had been assigned to Carter. She smiled in consolation. "Oh, Mama, I can tell this has been hard on you. I want you to know that we see tons of cases of infant RSV. In fact, this whole section becomes the RSV Wing each year about this time. Baby is going to be just fine and so are you."

What an enormous relief! The Oakes hospital staff had done everything they could, but they weren't prepared to handle Carter's case. My traumatization eased with their confidence and experience.

Carter spent four nights in the children's ICU.

This was a gut check for me. I knew how quickly the first year of an infant's passed because I'd experienced it with Andrew. Even with a full twelve-week maternity leave, I suddenly felt I wasn't getting enough time with our little guys.

# Flagpoles

After his run with RSV, Carter couldn't catch a break. His compromised immune system made him vulnerable to every bug that came along. He was sick all. The. Time. Just as he finished one antibiotic, he was put on another. Infections couldn't clear entirely or recurred.

I took a lot of time off and spent more days working from home than I should have so I could be with my baby. When I was home with him, I felt like I should be at work. When I was at work, I felt like I should be with my kids.

As if the mom guilt wasn't tough enough, I began struggling with the difference in leadership philosophy I had with the team I worked for. I finally made it to the Fargo office to train Marilyn's team. At the end of the training, she said, "Why don't you do more of this? It's your gift, Rebecca."

There it was again: my *gift*.

"It's not really in my specific job description," I replied.

"Isn't this why they hired you from Dale Carnegie? For your training skills?"

"I initially thought so, but they need a more business-oriented person to run the department," I said. "I would love to do more of this type of training. I think it's what the employees here really need. They need to be heard and they need to be valued."

Countless discussions with Marilyn followed, all regarding my role. While I appreciated her input, I always felt a bit deflated after our conversations because I knew I couldn't change the parameters of my job description. Training wasn't meant to be a big part of it. And I had had no idea how much I would miss doing it.

Charged with building a department, I put together a proposal that involved hiring several additional staff, growing it to a department of five. The women on my team were bright, fun, and mostly veteran employees of the company; in short, hiring them made me seem really smart. I prided myself on managing a department with open communication, transparency, and strong team chemistry because, in my mind, we could overcome any challenges with a strong culture.

I had never worked in the nonprofit world before and assumed most were mission- driven. Naively believing mission would trump politics, I figured our purpose would keep us focused and aligned. But I discovered that, no matter the industry, when you employ nearly 500 people and serve countless more, politics are always part of the game. I didn't do well with politics. I wanted straight talk. Open dialogue. No secrets. The amount of time, red tape, and bureaucracy involved with pushing a new idea forward was more than I was willing to take.

"Let's run it up the flagpole," they would say. I started to hate flagpoles.

One day, suffocated by the weight of work, I left my office to stroll around the grounds. I stood in the brilliant sunlight and tilted my face to the warm rays.

I just wanted to run. When I got an idea for my department and my team, I wanted to get the right people involved, get a solid plan in place, and run with it. But it wasn't that easy. I couldn't run because someone else had my shoes. Some other department had my route. My iPod? Someone had that, too. How could I pull my hair back? That's right. I had to ask someone for a ponytail holder.

I didn't have what I needed. I wasn't equipped to run. What was the point of being a department head if you had no real authority?

I loved my team, but being surrounded by great people wasn't enough to put me at ease when I felt equally surrounded by flagpoles.

## Holding It Together

In December, our family received another crushing blow; Lyle, my Fun Dad, had been diagnosed with lung cancer. A man who never smoked and who treated his body like a temple of the Lord, Lyle was the last person we expected to get cancer. As we waited to hear the prognosis, we all considered what this might mean. The Hankels were my parents' best friends and travel buddies. When Mom managed to gently nudge Dad off the farm, they usually traveled with Lyle and Noreen, building a catalog of their shenanigans. Lyle appreciated my husband's desert-dry, deadpan humor more than anyone else. Throw in a dose of Lyle's bizarre thought process and those two got all of us rolling in laughter. Lyle's boys and their families had to think of life without him.

Of course, none of us were as impacted by this initial news than Noreen. Of all the gifts Lyle bestowed on me as an impressionable young woman, the reverence he showed for his bride was probably the most moving. Lyle and Noreen had a holy, sacred, connected marriage, and the notion of life without him didn't exist in her mind.

After church on Christmas, I hugged him, holding him tighter and longer than normal. I started to cry a bit and so did he, but I only said, "Merry Christmas, Lyle."

Waiting to move into the new house we'd purchased, Jeremiah and I were staying with Mom and Dad for the interim. Like we always do, Mom and I got geared up to make this house ours. On a random Tuesday, Mom and I were painting when Dad called my cell phone. Lyle was expecting the results of his PET scan that day so Mom had been on edge the whole morning.

"Hi, honey. Is your mom there?" Dad asked.

"Yep, do you want me to get her?"

"No, but I wanted to tell you that I just got off the phone with Noreen. Lyle's results are not good. The doctors believe he'll have only six months with no treatment and up to a year with treatment. I think we should head over there to see them. Will you tell your mom that for me?"

"Yes, I'll tell her," I said in a near whisper.

Mom knew something was wrong before I even ended the call. "What? What did they find out?"

"Oh, Mom, it's not good." I tried to stem the quiver in my voice.

"No! No! No!" Mom shrieked as she dropped to her knees on the hardwood floor of my new kitchen. When her gut-wrenching sobs subsided enough for her to hear me, I gave her the full report.

She rose from the floor, swiping at her wet face with the backs of her hands. "I'm sorry to leave you, honey, but I need to go."

I hugged her fiercely and told her I loved her and that I was so, so sorry. I wasn't sure how she'd do it, but I knew she was preparing herself to put her head down and gut her way through this. Noreen needed her to be strong. Lyle needed her to be strong. So she did what she had to do; Mom went into management mode and handled it. Her own pain would have to wait.

# Prostitution

Not long after Lyle's prognosis, my boss called me into her office when I was on campus one day. "As part of our compensation review, we performed market surveys of all the positions within the organization and some of the positions were underpaid, according to the market. Your position was one of those. Here's your new salary based on the complexity of your role. It's not a retroactive adjustment, so you'll see the increase reflected in your next paycheck."

I looked at the numbers on the paper she slid across her desk. I earned a $15,000 pay increase!

*Holy shit!* I thought. *That's an incredible amount of money.* Why didn't I feel honored? Why did it feel like a slap in the face? What was my problem?

On the drive home, I figured it out: I felt like I was trading more than my time and energy for their money; I felt like I was trading my soul for their money. Now they offered me even more, presumably for more of my soul. To me, that sounded a lot like prostitution. Or, you know, what I could only assume prostitution felt like since I lacked firsthand experience.

Despite the increase in pay, I contemplated leaving. I had stopped being myself. I had started being the type of person that I couldn't stand and, ironically, trained others not to be.

In my mind, I heard the words I'd said to countless clients: "You always have choices. You can choose to work through your challenges with a positive attitude and stay, or you can leave. The only option you can't choose is to stay and be negative. It's not right to be a toxic person who poisons the workplace."

At this point, I was toxic. I was poisoning the well. I'd tried to work through my challenges. I'd talked myself blue to my boss and talked most often to Marilyn. She always said, "If you feel like this place is changing you, you need to get out before you lose yourself entirely."

But what about my team? I had recruited them from other departments and caused a lot of turmoil doing so. I couldn't just leave them without a leader. What would happen to them?

When I said that to Marilyn, she reminded me, "You can't stay in a job you don't love for other people. They are on their own journey. It's not your place to decide what's best for them. They need to decide for themselves."

In other words, I couldn't save them if I was drowning myself.

I had countless discussions with my parents; neither of them could fathom walking away from a job that paid so well and, at face value, seemed so flexible. But when I poured my torn, worn heart out to Mom, she knew it was taking its toll. She never once suggested I find my big girl panties or that I put my head down and get through it.

Dad acknowledged, "I can't imagine working for someone else. I've always been my own boss."

I missed calling the shots. I missed feeling like I was my own boss, in charge of my life and my happiness. I couldn't change the job to fit what I needed and I didn't want the place to change me, so I had no other option. I needed to leave.

As I watched my parents helping their nearest and dearest friends through Lyle's desperate fight, I was reminded about the fragility and uncertainty of tomorrow. I didn't want to waste time doing something that didn't feel right, because of money.

For the second time in my short career, I felt the crushing disappointment of my expectations not aligning with reality. I had thought once I was making great money in a challenging job, I'd feel set for life. I couldn't anticipate how much I would miss freedom and flexibility.

The past two years, I had only been free to help at Potters Way on weekends because of my job. My kids were growing up right before my eyes—and they were in daycare full-time. I didn't feel like I was truly serving anyone.

Jeremiah had settled into his new life in Oakes, as seamlessly as though *he* were the one who'd grown up there. From his slow pace, which I called his "mosey," to his one-finger farmer's wave at every passing car, Jeremiah belonged to this small town.

On the other hand, I was still trying to find my place. I thought this job would give me the best of both worlds. But my career wasn't going as planned and, without it, who was I? What was my value? Would I ever feel like the old Rebecca again?

I couldn't help feeling some resentment, as misplaced as it was. I secretly resented Jeremiah for securing his spot in the world.

He certainly wanted me to be happy. He knew that my work environment was taking a toll on me. I was short with the kids; my temper flared with him. The situation was changing me.

Even though he understood all of that, he still didn't really get it. "Beck, you're making so much money. You really want to just walk away from it? What's your plan?"

"I know I could call up Tonya and Tamara, and they'd take me back." Of that I was confident. "I also have an idea for a business I'd like to start eventually. I won't be replacing the income for a while, though."

"Well, you better get your plan in place," he said. "There are a lot of financial considerations to have worked out before you just up and quit your job."

He was right, but the confirmation of his support lifted a huge burden from my heart. I was worried about money, certainly, but until this point, I really had no idea how Jeremiah's business was doing financially. I managed our household finances, but I wasn't involved with the accounting side of his business. When we finished our taxes for the year and he told me what we owed, I nearly fell over. My husband was running an incredibly successful business. And I had barely acknowledged his success.

In my hustle to get my groove back, I had completely neglected Jeremiah and the progress of his business. I silently vowed that, along with spending more time with my children, as a result of this career move I'd make it a point to spend more time Jeremiah as well.

# Climbing Off

I started working my plan. I rejoined the Dale Carnegie team in February, facilitating for them to earn some replacement money. I explored our options for medical insurance. This didn't prove to be as hard as I originally thought. We got catastrophic coverage in place in the event of something, well, catastrophic. It wasn't ideal: our family premium was about the same price as our mortgage payment. But it was doable.

I tackled our monthly budget, painfully and tediously itemizing. *Everything.* I found $700 of expenses we could eliminate, one of which was an extra day of daycare for the boys. They could be home with me on Fridays, a positive for all of us.

Most importantly, I considered the looming financial question: What is the worst that can happen?

If I gave this a year and failed, was I unemployable? No, I was not. Would I be able to find another job? Sure.

The perfect one? Maybe, maybe not. But I would find something.

Finally, I selectively chose those with whom I would share my plans. And I prepared myself for the barrage of questions I knew I would get from them. I had always felt defined by my work and now here I was, jumping back off the ladder again. I knew others wouldn't understand.

Once I'd gently nudged Jeremiah to agree that it was time, I hopped off the ladder for the final time. My last day of employment was May 31.

A week later, Jeremiah came into the kitchen where I was starting dinner. "Hi, honey."

He smiled and pulled me close for a hug. "It's good to have my wife back."

I laughed. "Even if your wife is making us broke?"

"I'd rather you be broke and yourself than rich and miserable."

My husband was amazing. Lyle was right to like him as much as he did.

In October, I launched my blog, *How Mommy Got Her Groove Back*, and started writing about business and motherhood. It wasn't perfect. I wasn't ready. I didn't have all the answers and a clear business plan. To be truthful, I didn't have my groove back entirely. What I did have was a burning desire to find other women who felt like I felt.

My original concept was to create a village of woman business owners who lived in small communities, away from traditional networking opportunities. I envisioned a tribe of My People, women who identified with the loneliness and isolation of a small town but still had big dreams. I wanted to help them get their groove back. I launched my business during a customer service session I facilitated at a local women's business conference. Marilyn, who left her job a month earlier to step out in her own business, sat in the front row. It was a "coming out" party for the two of us.

Afterward she asked, "Was part of the session your content rather than Dale Carnegie's?"

"Yeah," I grinned. "I didn't love a lot of what I was finding in-house, but there were a couple of really great customer service books that I pulled from to put the second half together."

"Your whole demeanor and energy shifted when you switched to your stuff," she pointed out. "I know Carnegie brings you comfort. It's familiar and pays the bills, but consider whether you need to stay under that umbrella or if you can serve the world more by just being you."

"Why do you have to be so wise, Marilyn?" I joked. She had a habit of pushing me to see my gifts and find the courage to use them. I was off the ladder for good.

I started writing. I wrote about business, but it nearly always included motherhood because, as I now so painfully realized, there was no such thing as work-life balance. It was all just life.

Jeremiah and I had been in Oakes for five years. By design, few in my hometown had any inkling of what I did for work. I hadn't fully embraced living in a rural community and still felt as though my value came from work—and my best work was carried out anywhere other than in Oakes. It was a balancing act of a different kind. I kept one foot in Fargo, where I could see people and do work that felt the most like "me" and kept my other foot in Oakes so Jeremiah could have a business he was proud of and my kids would have the great upbringing I had.

I was trying to live two lives. Smart, driven, professional Rebecca had her big life in Fargo. Farmer's wife, country-loving daughter, and mom Becky had her home life in Oakes.

The ballad of my life now sounded dissonant. Just like unharmonious notes in a song demand resolution, so did my heart.

At Dale Carnegie, I didn't feel as relevant as I once had. I wasn't in corporate America anymore; I was a farmer's wife and mom. And I was self-employed at that. All the principles, content, and materials were in complete alignment with my beliefs about leadership. My uncertainty was about the context. There had to be a way I could blend my personal experiences with my professional expertise to have the same impact. There had to be. With no clear solution in sight, I was determined to figure it out.

As my blog gained traction, women began connecting and offering feedback. I realized I could help *all moms* and didn't need to focus solely on business or small towns. For the first time in my life, I was on a path of my own. There were no flagpoles in sight. If I wanted to make a change, I could. So I did.

*How Mommy Got Her Groove Back* underwent its first shift when I switched my focus to support all moms. Initially, this felt like the answer to my conflict with Dale Carnegie. Moms were the leaders of their households. I would tailor what I knew about leadership to them. I knew exactly what I wanted to offer first.

# Setting Boundaries

Thanks to guidance and assistance from Marilyn, the following January I nervously hosted my first event, The Busy Mom's Retreat. No longer operating this retreat under the umbrella of Dale Carnegie, I relied solely on my ideas. My material. My facilitation.

Eleven amazing mothers joined me at Coteaus des Prairie Lodge, located in *really* rural North Dakota. *Really* rural as in more rural than Oakes.

Merely three miles from South Dakota, the towering log cabin perched high on a ridge and offered a breathtaking view of the prairie, a welcome getaway from the hustle and bustle of motherhood. I created an itinerary that allowed mom attendees to escape their daily work and schedules, to focus on themselves. As it turns out, that was also hard work.

We kicked off the weekend with icebreaker activities followed by dinner. As I opened a bottle of wine, the vibe of connection was exactly as I hoped it would be. The women who came in as strangers were opening up and allowing themselves to be seen. Later that evening, Nicole—a dear friend from my youth who had also returned to Oakes—arrived. I had invited Nicole, a holistic chiropractor, to share her knowledge of oils during the two-hour block of free time I carved out for Saturday.

My heart skipped a beat. My breath caught. My mouth fell open.

Nicole was carrying her nine-month-old daughter.

My euphoric buzz died.

I shot Marilyn a look. The one she returned was nervous, nervous *for me*. Somehow, I found the words to greet Nicole.

Underlying the evening meal and activities was … baby noise. No crying. No screaming. Happy baby coos and gurgles—but noise just the same. At one point, one of the participants complained, "I came here to get away from those noises. She's a good little girl, but I just can't concentrate."

Ugh. I knew I was going to have to say something. It would have to wait until the next day.

I spent the night, tossing and turning, stressing over the situation. I knew Nicole was nursing Emersyn and probably couldn't be away from her at night. Who better than me to understand that quandary? I didn't sleep a wink. I didn't have a grandma on hand to soothe my sadness with baked goods. Thankfully, I did have a Marilyn.

Early Saturday morning, I traipsed to Marilyn's room for a pep talk.

"I have to say something to Nicole, don't I." My comment was more statement than question. I already knew what I had to do. I just held out hope she'd say it wasn't so.

"I'm sorry, but yes, you do."

My heart sank. I didn't want to hurt Nicole. I didn't have a single clue about what to say. Would this ruin our friendship? I dreaded approaching her.

Marilyn hugged me tightly. "You created this retreat to remind these moms to love themselves and show themselves compassion. Show Nicole that you love her enough to tell her the truth."

*Marilyn, for the win,* I thought. *Everyone needs a Marilyn.* I'd always sworn that she would be my perfect Sister Wife—and that together we'd hunt out a third wife who could cook.

After breakfast, I pulled Nicole—babe in arms—aside, into one of the bedrooms at the end of the hallway. I reached for her hand.

"I don't even know how to start this conversation. You know I love you, right? You know that I'd never say anything to intentionally hurt you, right?"

She looked startled. Worried.

I tenderly repeated the complaint I'd heard the night before. "Because people paid for this experience, it is my obligation to tell you that having Emersyn here is disrupting the retreat." I took a deep breath. "I am fully responsible, Nick, for not clearly stating anywhere in the marketing materials that children weren't allowed to attend. I'm sorry."

We discussed her options. She decided to call her husband and ask him to pick up the baby. I was grateful that she didn't choose to withdraw from the retreat; I wanted *her* to get something out of the weekend, too.

She cried. I cried. We hugged.

Nicole could have responded quite differently. She could have been angry and hurt. She could have un-friended me. Even though that would have been a horrible outcome, I was obligated to rectify the situation. It was right for all involved. A difficult conversation for me to initiate, it turned out to be highlight for all of us because it was real, honest, and filled with love.

The participants (and I) learned the importance of hard conversations.

That setting boundaries with people isn't easy, especially when it involves people we love dearly. That the fear of causing pain can cause us to suppress our thoughts. That when we fail to voice what we need and expect from them, we are holding others to unspoken standards that they'll never meet. That silence is acceptance.

## We Are Family

For Christmas, I gifted my cousin, Sara, a registration at The Busy Moms Retreat.

Sara and I had a complicated relationship. I loved her like a sister, but our friendship was not without its ups and downs. Sara had a rebellious streak; I was in the good girl lane. Less than a year apart in age, we chose different paths. She married earlier, had kids earlier, and while a hard-working dependable employee, never found a deep sense of value in her jobs. While I searched for the right ladder to climb, Sara focused on getting through the crazy toddler years with her two kids. Our lives were out of sync. She felt insecure around me; I kept up a façade of having it all together. In short, we hid our crazy from each other, just like we'd been taught to do.

The retreat was designed to force us to open up and share our true selves. I watched Sara become vulnerable and, in doing so, garner the love of the other participants. The closing activity on Sunday required each attendee to open her palms and accept positive feedback from the others. Her only job was to stand up and receive, uncharacteristic for moms who spend their days giving. To my dismay, the women urged me to participate, too. When I opened my hands, Sara was in line.

"Cousin, I always knew you were good at your job, but I never really knew what you did. I had no idea you had this in you. I had no idea you were capable of this." Her eyes brimmed. "I'm so, so proud of you, and I'm proud to be your cousin."

Sara and I had finally, fully connected. We fully showed up for each other, vowing never to fall out of sync again. We were family and family is everything. At long last, Sara became a forever Nestie.

Pondering the weekend on the drive home, I realized that I had arrived—I had found my place. I was where I was meant to be. Moms needed each other, and I could offer a place of safety and refuge for them to grow and connect. I was excited for the future of my business.

## Back in the Trenches

A month later, Jeremiah and I made an impromptu trip to Fargo to take the boys swimming at a hotel, something you do to cope with never-ending North Dakota winters. Sara, Nathan, and their kids joined us for a night of swimming and eating pizza.

The next morning as I brushed my teeth, I was sucker-punched with a sobering thought. *My period is late.* When I mentioned it to Jeremiah, his response was calm and casual.

"I'm sure it's nothing. Your period has always been irregular. We'll get a test for you when we stop at Target."

*He's right,* I thought. *There's no way I'm pregnant now.*

I'd learned my lesson several years earlier and bought a digital test. No more faintly pink lines or I-can't-tell-if-that's-a-plus-sign. When the magic stick of altered destinies displayed the singular word I was hoping to not see, I looked in the mirror. The granddaddy of all curse words slipped out of my mouth. One little f-word. So much feeling.

Pregnant. With our third baby.

Laughter and tears overwhelmed me simultaneously in an awkward, lump-in-the-stomach, Jekyll and Hyde kind of moment. Excited and terrified, I felt helpless.

This was unplanned. This was unexpected. This was alarming. This was God's way of reminding me that I'd never been, nor would I ever be, in control.

Jeremiah and I had been firmly on the fence about having a third child. Our two little boys were almost five and three. Life was getting markedly easier. Now, we'd be back in the trenches. How did I really feel about this?

To me, the world didn't seem designed for families of five. Roller coasters. Motel rooms. Twix candy bars. Our family vehicle. Board games. There would always be a poor kid left out because everything is easier in pairs. Not to mention, I only had two arms.

My new business was just finding legs. How would a third child affect it? Andrew was born in spring during Jeremiah's busy season. I had delivered Carter in late summer during Mom's frantic crunch-time to get ready for the pumpkin patch. This baby? This baby was due on *opening day* of Potters Way that fall. I would be largely without Mom's or Jeremiah's support. I'd already received a ton of grief because of the timing of the first two. People thought a farmer's wife should have been capable of better planning. Now what would they think?

What about the bikini body I was planning to acquire?

How would I make it a full nine months without an alcoholic beverage?

As I subconsciously completed the cons list on the right-hand side of my mental T-chart, I realized it didn't matter how I felt, how we felt. We were having a third baby.

Deep down, I knew there was room in my heart for one more. Plus, we would get another shot at parenting. And who knew? Maybe we'd have a girl this time.

## "Love Your Husband"

While our world brimmed with new-baby excitement, Lyle and Noreen and their family were coming to grips with Lyle's prognosis. Although he'd surpassed doctors' expectations, the cancer had spread to his spine, with pinpricks evident in his brain—despite a year of chemotherapy and radiation treatments.

With the end near, I decided to drive to the assisted living facility in Fergus Falls, Minnesota, to tell him goodbye. My parents firmly believed I shouldn't see Lyle in his current state; I should remember him as he used to be.

"I get it, Mom, I really do," I said into the phone. "But I need to see him. I wrote him a letter last week, but I need to see him in person. To say goodbye."

"We won't stop you, but prepare yourself. He doesn't look like he did when you saw him last."

As Jeremiah and I made the two-and-half-hour drive, my heart was heavy. I reminisced, telling my husband childhood stories he'd never heard or was too caring to admit he's heard before. At Broen Home, we asked for directions but dawdled down the hall, slowed by apprehension.

Approaching his room, we overheard Noreen talking to Pastor O'Brien and his wife, Audrey, so we hesitated before entering. When we walked through the door, the weight of the inevitable was pronounced. After a round of hugs and greetings, we engaged in small talk until everyone left us with Lyle.

Jeremiah knew I needed a moment alone with my beloved Fun Dad. After he left, I edged onto the bed with Lyle and reached for his hands. As I leaned in, I noticed his thin frame, frail appearance, drawn face. But I wasn't frightened. I didn't dwell on the obvious changes. When we locked eyes, his appearance didn't matter.

"Hi, Lyle." I put my forehead on our clasped hands, trying to hide the emotion that overwhelmed me.

"Beck, don't cry," he said, his voice frail. "It's okay."

Even on his deathbed, he was more worried about me.

"You know how much you mean to me, don't you?" I searched his face for confirmation. "You know how much I love you, right?"

"Yes, and I love you, too," he whispered.

I sat with him for several minutes, silently willing him to feel my love. A chatty kid who had grown into a chatty woman, for the life of me, I couldn't find any words. I didn't know what to say. I had never broached the topic of cancer with him. Maybe I feared that acknowledging it would be an admission that he might not get through it. Cancer sucked and it was snatching a wonderful soul from this earth. It wasn't fair. Yet I couldn't say that to Lyle. He already knew it.

When Noreen ushered in another visitor, I knew my precious moments with Lyle were over. I kissed his forehead, my tears dampening his hair. "I'll see you again, Lyle. I love you." I repeated myself to make sure he heard me and believed me.

When Noreen walked us to the hallway, we held each other, desperate and resigned. "What can I do for you, Noreen? Is there anything you need, anything I can do?" I knew she had family in Fergus Falls to support her. And my mom.

Mom had always been a nurturer, but I'd never seen her handle something of this scope or magnitude. Whereas Lyle had always been Noreen's rock, Mom took over the role while Noreen prepared herself for his death. For Mom, it was sacred work. I'd never admired her more in my entire life.

Noreen pulled back from our hug, looked me in the eye, and tearfully gripped my shoulders. "What you can do is go home and love your husband. Honor him and tell him every day you love him."

She saw the look of surprise on my face. "Beck, I mean it."

"I will," I promised. And I, too, meant it.

Fun Dad died on Easter Monday, surrounded by his family. I hugged my family a little tighter and remembered to tell Jeremiah I loved him.

## Daughter Doubts

During prior pregnancies we didn't know the sex, but with this surprise baby, my Type-A, controlling, inner-perfectionist demanded the right to plan *something*. To our utter delight, we discovered at our twenty-two week ultrasound that we were expecting a baby girl. Joyous and grateful, I took a moment to revel in the knowledge that God, of course, had The Plan for our family, and this little miss was meant to be a part of it.

While I was completely thrilled, I felt serious trepidation. This wasn't the girls-are-sassier-and-won't-like-you-for-a-large-chunk-of-their-youth kind of anxiety. With the boys, I was off the hook; Jeremiah was their model. This didn't diminish my role, but I knew they would learn how to be a man from Jeremiah, not me. Now, I'd be raising a daughter. I'd be her primary role model.

I knew what I was like as a child, how much I pushed Mom's buttons. How on earth was I stable enough to raise a daughter and help her manage all her emotions? I suddenly became aware of the changes I needed to make in my life.

No more complaining about thunder thighs and bitching that my boobs weren't big enough. My daughter needed an example of positive body image. I would have to accept my own, think of it as beautiful, and practice gratitude for all it did for me—a little message with a big impact. The last thing I wanted was a five-year-old refusing a piece of chocolate because she was watching her weight.

No more perfectionism. My daughter needed a fearless role model, a mother willing to accept flaws. I should ease up on being so self-critical when I screwed up. I wanted my little girl to embrace risk-taking without fear of making mistakes or looking stupid. I wanted to show her the value in trying new things without needing to be awesome at everything.

No more caring what others thought about me—which had plagued me all my life. My daughter should have a confident role model. I would have to stop struggling with my strengths which, I feared, others misdiagnosed as bitchy and bossy. I could hear myself saying one day, "What other people think of you is none of your business, honey." She would roll her eyes and tell me I'm lame. Chances were good that this baby would have a fire in her spirit. I'd find it cosmically unlikely for her to be any other way.

So, I concluded, this daughter and I would be bitchy together. And dramatic. And probably a little bossy. But, the goal was to teach her to be confident, proud of her choices and the person she would become … providing her choices weren't morally bankrupt or illegal.

Here I'd been spouting to moms that we ultimately teach our children by our actions, not our words. It was time to put my money where my mouth was. Yikes. This baby was only twenty-three weeks in utero and I needed a handbook: *You're Having a Daughter and You Already Feel Like a Failure.*

Although stressed over the idea of raising (and potentially ruining) a daughter, I could always rely on Marilyn's wisdom: "I paid for my own therapy; my kids can pay for theirs."

# Meltdown

Spring was always difficult for me as a mom. The fickle weather and ever-muddy conditions from snowmelt and frost made it difficult to enjoy being outside with the kids. If Jeremiah obsessed over anything, it was planting in the spring. As my dad said, "When the ground is fit, you go." With selling, treating, and delivering seed to his customers, Jeremiah was rarely around, leaving me to shoulder the complex roles of mom, dad, plumber, carpenter, cook, gardener …. Whatever the demand, I tried to fill it.

The spring of my third pregnancy was the most difficult since moving back to Oakes, especially irritating because my perfectionism gene—on high alert—insisted I should be better at this gig, not worse. The day-to-day tasks of managing the household, balancing my business with keeping the boys alive, and growing a new little being left me feeling inadequate.

Actively engaged in the delight of adding a nursery to our home, I was caught up in details and decisions. But I had no one to share it with. No one to bounce ideas off of. No one to … talk to. Working from home isolated me from people. Adult people; my kids didn't count. I struggled being alone for large amounts of time with only my thoughts for company.

One particular Saturday, I woke to rain—which provokes one of two responses in farm wives: you're delighted to spend extra time with your farmer or you're irritated that they're in the way, messing up your plans!

While typically in the second camp, that morning I was genuinely excited. I pictured us talking, visiting, sharing, and brainstorming remodeling ideas. I imagined us hanging out with the kids, laughing and playing. Cooking meals together and ending our day with a long snuggle on the couch while we watched a movie we'd both wanted to see and shared a communal bucket of popcorn, because that's what a couple who really loved each other did.

Sometimes, I set myself up for a mild amount of disappointment.

Tired, Jeremiah slept in. Meanwhile I got the kids up, fixed breakfast, and played with them. By late morning, I decided to rouse Jeremiah and start fulfilling my version of the day.

Well, let's just say my visualization technique didn't work. Annoyed that I was bombarding him with questions and plans for the nursery, he interrupted. "Do we have to do this right now?"

"Are you kidding me? When else can we talk about it? You haven't been around to talk to!" Pent up feelings and resentment flowed. So did my ever-ready tears.

"Now you're crying? There is nothing to cry about. Just quit fretting about all of this."

Hormonal and emotionally spent, I walked from our bedroom and into the bathroom. Door firmly closed, light off, I sprawled on the floor and bawled, all the while embracing my burgeoning stomach because I feared my unborn baby could feel my intense despair.

*I take care of everything around here. How dare he tell me not to cry and fret!* I didn't want to be a farmer's wife anymore. I didn't want this life. I couldn't bring another baby into this world. This chaos. This mess. I couldn't even handle what I had.

I was a failure.

*Why can't I get my shit together? I wish I could just get in my car and leave. But where would I go? Where can I go? I need to talk to someone, but who I can trust with all of this?*

I peeled myself from the bathroom floor and told Jeremiah that I was leaving, smugly vindicated when he looked a bit terrified—possibly because I said "leaving" like I wasn't coming back.

"Wait, what?" He sat up in the bed, his eyes wide.

Softening a fraction, I said, "I just need to go for a drive."

"Look, I'm sorry. Please don't go." He tried to embrace me.

I pulled away and walked out. I just needed to—go.

Backing out the driveway, with no aim or direction, I headed south out of town. Oakes being only 1.6 square miles, within minutes I found myself surrounded by open fields and few houses. The country was a perfect place to wallow in self-pity.

I ran down a mental list of people I could share my feelings with. I couldn't tell my mom. My farmer's wife struggles were laughable compared to what she endured when I was young. I couldn't tell anyone in Oakes; articulating my feelings would lead to misunderstandings, which would lead to rumors and gossip about me divorcing my husband.

I decided to call Marilyn, my font of wisdom who never judged. I pulled the car over and dug in my purse for my cellphone.

Marilyn listened. She let me feel like I did. She let me just be who I was in that moment. She let me know I wasn't alone.

Here's what she *didn't* do:

She didn't say, "Why don't you just stop worrying? You should feel grateful that you have a husband. You should feel grateful that you have a healthy pregnancy. You should …"

Here's what she *did* do:

She said, "You're okay. We've all been there and you're okay."

Blessed Marilyn knew exactly what I needed. I drove home, found my big girl panties, and carried on.

The incident reminded me that no one has it completely together. We are human. We screw up. And sometimes when we do, we think ugly, nasty thoughts and we feel ugly, nasty things.

My entire life, I'd been the biggest "feeler" in my immediate family. Even as a grown woman, I sometimes struggled to communicate my feelings, somehow believing they had to make sense. I often put on a good face and pretended everything was okay. This meltdown and Marilyn's gracious response made me realize that I couldn't force myself to feel one way or the other.

I understood that when I struggled, it did me no good to wish I were different. As a Type-A individual, I had a little (undiagnosed) OCD; I was a bit of a control freak; and I had really big feelings. Sometimes this served me, sometimes it didn't.

These distinct facets of my personality were just as much a part of me as my gender and height. Trying to pretend I was different was like denying that I was a woman. Or that I was tall.

Life would always throw me curveballs. Sometimes, I'd want to run away. Sometimes, my personality won't serve me well. *But,* I determined, *I will reach out to the people in my life who will stand with me in my dark moments, never suggesting that the answer is to be less "me."*

Because that was about as pointless as asking me to be petite.

# The Big Shift

As the summer continued, I spent little time on my business. I felt preoccupied with the impending arrival of our daughter and anxious about another major milestone soon on the horizon. Andrew would start kindergarten in August.

I don't know why, but the anticipation of this event made me feel *unhinged*. As my belly grew and my time with my little boy disappeared, I became even more emotionally raw. Hormones were a tricky thing.

We also had to squeeze in Carter's third birthday. We celebrated on a Sunday with some of our good friends and their kids, making Carter feel special. It was important to me that he felt like he mattered, knowing that his little world would be rocked when our daughter arrived.

Tuesday was Andrew's first day of school. I couldn't stop staring as he ate his breakfast at the counter. He caught me looking at him and asked, "Mom, are you okay?"

"I just can't believe you're going to school." He had grown up before my eyes.

"Are you going to cry?" He knew me all too well.

My answer was honest. "Maybe."

With precious innocence, he asked, "Is that because you think I won't do well in school?"

"Oh, buddy, of course you're going to do well! I might cry because I'm sad I won't have as much time with you anymore." I almost started to cry just saying the words out loud.

Before loading into the car, we took the momentous first day of school pictures in front of our house and with the other neighborhood kids (his "other" brothers and sisters). After dropping Carter off at daycare, we made the trek to school.

The hum of our little town was practically audible, a stark difference to the quiet summer when so many people vacate Oakes for the lake season. We parked the car a block away and walked toward the elementary building.

The memories of my own school days came rushing in as we walked through the "flagpole entrance" of the elementary school. Kids, teachers, and parents flooded the halls. We located Andrew's classroom, where we were greeted by his teacher, Mrs. Pederson, who helped him find the hook for his backpack and the cubby for his school supplies. I took a picture of the two of them before it was time for me to say goodbye.

I escorted Andrew down the hall to the door leading to the playground where he would spend the first part of his morning. Bending over my swollen belly, I looked him in the eye. "Buddy, have an awesome first day of school." I squeezed him harder than usual.

He smiled up at me brightly. "Okay, Mom! See you after school!"

I released him from my embrace and watched my very small boy walk onto the very big playground. The tears I'd successfully held back finally brimmed over. My chiropractor friend Nick saw me and came over to give me a quick hug. I was not the only mama crying in the hallway that first day.

As I turned away, our neighbor and church friend Tara burst down the hallway, loudly proclaiming, "Last first day of school for us! Woo-hoo!" She had just dropped off the youngest of her five children at kindergarten.

I laughed out loud.

She looked at me and grinned. "It does get easier!"

*Thank God for a good sense of humor and great people who remind me to laugh.*

As I waddled back to the car, I felt another shift. And no, it wasn't my baby girl who was running out of room in the inn. Something shifted in my heart. This moment had arrived so swiftly that it truly caught me off guard. I hadn't realized how quickly five beautiful years with my sweet boy would fly. I suddenly felt I'd missed out on time with him.

With a new baby coming so quickly on the heels of this experience, I was questioning many of the things I always thought to be true.

Could I really "have it all?" Had I been chasing a fantasy? What if my career wasn't the only place I offered value? In my pursuit to "figure it all out," had I been missing out on the best moments with my family? Had I been pursuing a plan wasn't meant for me anymore? What did I really want? What really mattered to me?

Who was I—really?

## Anxious Anticipation

As my due date approached, my anxiousness grew. The Oakes hospital no longer handled deliveries, so I drove the inconvenient eighty-five miles to Jamestown (where Jeremiah's family lived) for all my appointments. Concerned that I might not make it to the hospital in time (I delivered Carter less than an hour after my water broke, we consulted my beloved Dr. Sorlie at my thirty-eight-week appointment.

"Stick with our plan. If your water breaks, get on the road," she said.

*Really?*

I'd been plagued by nightmares of delivering in the back of our car on the interstate. Even under those circumstances, Jeremiah would be a rock star. Rational and levelheaded, he would try to calm me. But if I popped out a baby, he already admitted he would farmerize the situation by zip-tying the umbilical cord. Good grief.

A looming concern was my lack of a support system. Although I had done what I could to help Mom get ready at Potters Way, I knew she would be caught up in her business for the next four weeks. But, what about me and my new baby? Jeremiah would be in the field. Of course there were a lot of others to help. I "only" needed to reach out. To ask.

Another layer of stress was the certain change a third child would bring. We had a pretty good thing going in our household, and the idea of impending sleepless nights and lack of dependable schedule boggled my mind.

"Are you excited?" people asked.

I stumbled to answer. Sure I was. *But, I like order. And babies are chaos.* What could I say? I had to tread lightly. People didn't want to hear that I wasn't one-hundred-percent stoked. They wanted me to beam with pride and glow with anticipation. Well, my glow was sweat, anxiety-induced sweat. Standing firmly outside my comfort zone, I knew I was being challenged to grow.

So what did a Type-A, perfectionist, control freak woman like me do to calm the beast inside her? I reminded myself that my biggest fears were unlikely to occur. My energy was limited; I couldn't afford to exert any by worrying and fretting.

And. I. Prayed.

Prayer was one of the pillars of my sanity at this point. God had brought me to this place and I knew He would carry me through it. Oh, I knew I couldn't put this all on God. In answer to the inappropriate question my dad often asked expectant mothers, yes, I knew how babies were made. A fun night away in Fargo was all it took and, while it wasn't on my radar, it happened because we let it. I asked God to remind me of the incredible blessings babies bring. The truth is, I had never been a good newborn mom. I preferred them at four months when they developed a routine. I *loved* routines.

So, I prayed for strength. I prayed for support. I prayed for peace. I prayed for confidence. I prayed. In the end, all would be as God meant it to be. I just had to roll with it. There was nothing left to do but throw my hands in the air and try to enjoy the ride.

## Brynlee and a Buffalo

Sitting in Tracie's hairdresser chair with heat blowing on my newly foiled head, I felt a sharp cramp in my stomach and gasped.

Tracie frowned and furrowed her forehead. "Are you okay?"

"Yeah, I am, but I think I'm going to leave for Jamestown tonight," I decided in the moment.

She nodded. "I think that would make you feel a lot better."

I left the salon and phoned Mom. "Could you take the boys home with you tonight?"

"Are you in labor?" She sounded worried.

"No, but I'll feel better in Jamestown. I want to go up tonight and stay with Jim and Teri so I can try to get some sleep."

"I think that's a good idea, honey."

Jeremiah agreed with my idea, so I tossed my suitcase in the car and drove straight to Jim and Teri's house. When I walked in the door that evening, the weight of an anvil lifted from my chest. I slept peacefully for the first time in nearly six weeks.

The next morning, Jeremiah joined me for my thirty-nine-week appointment. I was thankful this day had finally arrived because, from this moment forward, we had a game plan.

As she checked me, Dr. Sorlie declared, "Well, baby girl's head is locked and loaded. There's no chance of her floating back up, so here's what I'm thinking. If you want me to strip your membranes, we can do that. Then you just walk around today as much as possible and try to get labor moving on its own. If by Monday morning you haven't had the baby, I can break your water and we know you'll move quickly."

*I'm not leaving Jamestown without a baby!* I thought. *Thank you, Lord.* No more anxiety for me. We agreed with her plan.

"Now, don't get your hopes up that anything will happen. Stripping membranes only gets labor moving in about half of pregnancies."

I threw my arms around her in glee. At every appointment, I'd expressed my concern about being in Oakes. A no-bullshit doctor, she never made me feel like my fears were unwarranted; I delivered babies fast and eighty-five miles was a long distance to trek.

Jeremiah and I went about our day. We walked around Jamestown and even visited the National Buffalo Museum. The grounds conjured memories of Grandpa and Grandma Seefeldt taking ten-year-old me, Joe, Sara, and Sadie on a weekend road trip to Medora, a summertime tourist attraction in the westernmost part of the state. In an era before DVD players, Gameboys, and cell phones, we entertained ourselves with board games in the car.

Along the way, Grandpa stopped in Jamestown for us to stretch our legs. Treasured family photographs from the trip show us four kids standing under the giant buffalo in Jamestown. Now, there I was with my husband and my percolating baby, standing under the same buffalo.

Cramping and contractions accompanied me throughout the day but slowed by evening. I knew she wasn't coming yet.

*Come on, baby girl,* I urged. *We are so ready for you.*

Because I didn't want to disturb anyone if I was up a lot at night, I slept on the couch in the basement while Jeremiah slept upstairs in Teri's guest room. Around 4 a.m., I awoke to a painful contraction. It was long enough and painful enough to urge me to get up, brush my teeth, and start putting my stuff together. As soon as I grabbed my toiletry bag, I had another one and I felt the familiar soft pop of my water breaking.

*This is it! We better get moving!*

I took my bags upstairs, walked down the hallway to the guest room, and shook Jeremiah awake. "It's time. My water broke."

Now, I've already said it—Jeremiah moseys. We have always operated at different speeds. It did my heart good to see my man jump up out of bed with lightning speed, get his stuff together, and load us up in the car. He meant business.

The ten-minute drive to the hospital was easy since there was no traffic at that hour. Dr. Sorlie had instructed us to call the hospital to alert them because of my history of fast deliveries.

Jeremiah handled this situation like a boss. He spoke with authority, demanding they meet us at the ER entrance, perfectly following Dr. Sorlie's advice. As I was wheeled to the delivery room, I knew exactly what to do. No more thinking and fretting; it was time to put my head down and gut my way through this.

The delivery was fast and textbook as far as Dr. Sorlie was concerned, but it was wicked painful. When Jeremiah told Dr. Sorlie and the nurse about our venture to the buffalo, just as the baby's head crowned, I wanted to haul off and beat him senseless. They were discussing a buffalo while I was ready to push out a baby? Seriously?

As soon as our perfect baby was out and laying on my chest, Jeremiah looked straight at me and asked, "Are we done?"

"Yes. We are done. We are complete," I replied through my tears. I couldn't fathom going through it again.

Brynlee Jean was here. To my shock and surprise, after I exited the shower a few hours after delivering, my very first visitor walked in. Mom.

"I had no idea you were coming!" Now it felt real. My mom was here.

She had been in Valley City for a care conference for Gary, so it was easy to slip over and visit before heading home to work at the shop. She was *the best* surprise. Sharing a brand new, perfect baby with my mother was the only part of the delivery experience I thought I might miss with Brynlee being our last. All of my fretting, all of my worry, and all of my anxiety melted away.

Things had happened exactly as they needed to. I couldn't have planned this birth experience to happen more perfectly. As had happened so many times before, I was not so gently reminded that the notion of my control was an illusion. I needed to learn to trust the One who was in control. He never gets it wrong.

## Practicing Grace

With Brynlee, I hoped and prayed to persevere through nursing and to write an amazing post on my blog to encourage other moms to keep trying in spite of prior issues. The blog gave me a mantle of responsibility to my readers. Mommy bloggers do what's best for their kids. And clearly, nursing is the best, and good moms do it.

Despite my hopes for nursing redemption, that wasn't mean to be my story.

That's right. First, I was shaken down with Andrew. Then, I was confident with Carter. Now, I was a basket case again with Brynlee. But, really, *that* is what motherhood felt like. Moment to moment, my confidence ebbed and flowed. Along with my sanity. And my willpower to deny chocolate.

To put it mildly, I struggled. When I started nursing Brynlee in the hospital, I felt we were off to the best start I'd ever had. By day four, my milk had rushed in and her latch wasn't great; she had broken my nipple open. In the middle of the night, I tried to feed her an ounce of formula because she never seemed satisfied, but it took me twenty minutes to get her to take the bottle. The panic I felt was palpable and I nearly lost my mind.

In just a few short days, Jeremiah would be starting *harvest*. I'd be flying solo. Sunup to sundown and, obviously, the nights in between, I'd be on my own. I'd be getting two children up and out the door each morning. Alone. Well, not alone. I'd have an infant, too.

I knew then and there that this wasn't going to work for me and, once again, I grappled with shame.

The things I told myself that led to the shame: I'm a smart woman. All the research points to nursing as the only option smart women make. I'm not a quitter. I'm not a wimp. I delivered all three of my babies without drugs. I should be able to handle a little boob pain. I do things "right" and the right thing to do is to nurse. *What kind of a mom does it make me that I'm choosing the "less healthy" option for my baby?*

The things I felt that were hard to ignore: Trapped. Broken. Defective. Suffocated. Panicked. Frustrated. Unscheduled. Not bonded to my baby. Anxious. Resentful of my baby. Sad. Guilty. Shameful.

It seemed that as long as I had a good reason that nursing didn't work, like getting thrush with Andrew, people were generally very understanding of my reason to quit nursing. People are much less forgiving when they don't feel you have a valid reason.

Our first week home, Marilyn visited. I bawled as I shared my woe. She simply asked, "If Brynlee was a new mom and expressed these same feelings to you, what would you tell her? Would you tell her to suck it up? To stop being so selfish?"

I sniffled. "No, I'd tell her that wanting to quit doesn't mean she's a terrible mother." *In short, I'd want her to find true encouragement and support from me like I got from my mom when Andrew was a baby.*

Bingo. Hammer, meet the nail head. Even though I still had doubts, I gave up nursing within the first week and never looked back. I needed a friend like Marilyn to remind me that I must show myself grace. In my toughest moments, I needed to think of myself as a friend—to me.

# A New Chapter

Once I stopped nursing Brynlee, I found a rhythm to mothering three little kids. The boys adored their baby sister, evidenced by their enthusiastic race to her bedroom each morning to chatter at her through the railings of her crib.

I reflected back on my early days with Andrew, remembering how the days *dragged*. Between Andrew's new school schedule, Carter's daycare routine, and an infant, the hours flew. Plus, we spent as much time as we could out at the farm.

Mom made the tough decision to open Potters Way for her final season a week after Brynlee's birth. Originally, she planned to operate her business for ten years. In true perfectionist form, she felt bound by the contract she made with herself.

But with all she'd suffered through that year—Lyle's death, supporting Noreen as she struggled to find her new normal without him—Mom felt the pull to be free from the constraints of her business. Even though it was seasonal in nature, her business was as demanding as farming at times, success hinging on favorable weather conditions. As my parents knew all too well, Mother Nature was a temperamental lady, making it impossible to know what kind of crop you'd get from year to year.

I had a third baby. Being a grandma was my mother's greatest joy and she felt that she couldn't be there for us like she wanted to.

Lastly, she was truly starting to feel her age. She was tired. For the first time, she could see the difference in age between her and Dad. The preparations necessary to run her business were labor intensive, and she worried about the strain on him.

So, after seven years, she'd decided that this would be her final season. When Brynlee was two weeks old, we trekked to the farm with her older brothers in tow to meet our extended family and help Mom. I knew it was the right decision and fully supported the end of this chapter in her life. But I mourned the end of the business that had brought Mom and me together like nothing else could have. Potters Way brought Jeremiah and I back to Oakes and created timeless memories for our family and many of the families we loved in our community.

It was time for Mom to move on. She had her own groove to find.

## Mom to the Rescue

While ushering in a new year and preparing our tax returns, I was painfully aware of how big a financial decision I'd made when I left my nonprofit position. I had gone from my highest paying job to making the least amount of money I'd made since graduating from college. I'd hit rock bottom. Could I ever afford great shoes again?

Even though life was more complicated with three kids, I was excited to throw myself back into my new business. February was a big month. I was starting my first Dale Carnegie Course right in my own backyard. Although I had significantly scaled back my commitment with Dale Carnegie, Tonya and Tamara continued to champion me and support my work.

Scheduled to emcee a mom's event in Fargo on the seventh, I was caught up in plans for my next Busy Mom's Retreat slated for March. Dani and Sheri, owners of the regional magazine, *On the Minds of Moms*, were hosting the event. After attending my first Busy Mom's Retreat, they added this live event to their vision board. I was honored to emcee.

The best part about this gig was that they didn't over-script me; I had talking points, but they trusted me to set the right tone for the whole day. I adored Dani and Sheri and sincerely wanted them to have an amazing event. Viewing it as my comeback gig, I felt excitement—with a large dose of pressure to get it right.

On Tuesday the week of the event, my parents returned from a trip to St. Thomas sponsored by one of the seed companies Dad and Jeremiah represented. They came over to tell us about their adventure. Suddenly, Mom remembered, "Oh, your big event is this Saturday, isn't it? Do you need anything from me?"

"No, I don't think so," I replied. I didn't realize that, although she had already calendared the event, she was asking about specific expectations I had.

On Thursday, I called Mom to see if I could bring the kids a little earlier on Friday so I could leave town with more time to gear up for the next day.

"Oh, you need me to watch the kids this weekend? We made plans with our friends for dinner on Saturday night," she replied. "I've had to cancel on them a few times before, so I'd rather not cancel on them again."

"What?" I shrieked. "What do you mean? I'm counting on you to watch them! I asked you about this over six months ago! I wouldn't have agreed to the event in the first place if I wasn't certain I had the kids figured out first."

Panic gripped my heart. Jeremiah wasn't available. Kelsey, our incredible go-to babysitter, wasn't available. I didn't know who would watch the kids. Brynlee was only four months old. I didn't trust just anyone with her.

"Well, I asked you on Tuesday and you said you didn't need me." Her tone was defensive.

"I didn't know what you meant," I began. "I've had this on my calendar for months, Mom."

"Well, you can't expect everyone else to think about it as much as you do. Just because it's been on your mind for months doesn't mean it's been on mine."

"I can't even…" My voice trailed off as the fury built in my chest. "I have to go."

I hung up and screamed out loud. I hadn't been this angry with my mother since I screamed *I hate you* as a kid. I was so disappointed. And completely stressed out.

A few minutes later, she called back and asked if taking the kids on Friday, keeping them overnight, and then bringing them back before she and Dad went out on Saturday would help at all.

I thought, *No! That's not going to help me! I still need someone for Saturday and I don't want to try to piece a new plan together! I already had a plan!*

"No, we'll figure it out," I snapped and hung up the phone.

When I told Jeremiah, he offered to watch the kids. The only problem was, he wanted me to stay home until the kids were almost in bed because he didn't do well with Brynlee. I wouldn't get to Fargo until nearly 10 the night before the event.

Frustrated that Mom had flaked out on me and wasn't available and that Jeremiah was restricting me, I felt hurt and frazzled. Let down. Friday night, Jeremiah finally agreed, begrudgingly, to let me leave around 6:45. Brynlee was decently scheduled but she still had moments when she wasn't happy and, truthfully, he had just not been around enough to know her like I did. He didn't know how to comfort her when she was upset.

I was on Interstate 94 about seven miles outside of Fargo when Jeremiah called. I could hear Brynlee screaming in the background. "She hasn't stopped crying since you left," he said flatly.

"Well, give her a bottle and put her down for the night," I said. "She's probably just tired."

"She won't take her bottle. She won't eat it at all."

A surge of stress coursed through my body. "What do you want me to do about it?" I screeched. "I'm only ten minutes from Fargo!" I waited for a response. Nothing. "Do I have to call Mom?"

*Please just handle this, Jeremiah. Don't make me call Mom.*

"Yes, I guess, if you think that's best."

I had no idea what I thought was best! I hung up on him.

I hadn't talked to Mom since our spat, except for a quick phone call to tell her I had it figured out. I fumed, but placed the call.

"Mom, I need your help," I pleaded. I gave her the quick and dirty.

"Okay, I'll head into town for Jeremiah."

"Thanks."

"Mom's on her way in," I said to Jeremiah when I phoned him back. "I'm going to have a drink with Sara. I hope the rest of the night goes better."

As I drove into Fargo, a memory bolted through me, a story Mom told. I was one year old when she asked Dad to watch us kids while she went into town to help Grandpa and Grandma with the grand opening of their new store. They had purchased a new building and remodeled it. There was a ton of work to do and Mom really wanted to help. After about an hour, Dad called the store and told her she needed to come home. He couldn't handle me.

*How was it possible that I married a man who couldn't handle his own children?* In Jeremiah's defense, because his work kept him away from the house, he and Brynlee didn't really know each other. Also, he had given me fair warning. He told me he couldn't handle her. I just didn't want to believe him. *This is why I was never going to marry a farmer.*

Minutes later, when I sidled between Sadie and Sara at a restaurant bar in downtown Fargo, Sara slid a shot in front of me. I had called her earlier, in the wake of my panic and fury, to find out where we were meeting. I hugged her fiercely. She pulled away, ordering, "Drink it."

I tossed back my drink and did my best to relax into the evening. Whatever was going to happen at home couldn't be my problem anymore. But I certainly felt better knowing Mom had come to the rescue.

## Real Deal Reneé

I was especially eager to meet the event's opening keynote speaker, Reneé Rongen. Some time back, she and I had spoken by phone after her cousin, who had attended one of my Dale Carnegie courses, thought we should connect. During the phone call, she had said, "I love making people laugh and I'm good at it. I'm really funny on stage."

*What kind of person says that out loud?* I wondered. It seemed bold to be so self-assured.

When I arrived at the hotel for my sound check, I met Reneé in person. We chatted as I helped her place her materials on the tables. She was warm, personable, and funny.

"What kind of coaching services do you offer?" I asked. My business needed a boost and while I knew I'd never hire her without hearing her first, I thought I should try to get some information upfront.

Her answer was noncommittal. "I don't take on many clients because it's very time-consuming. My job is to hold people's feet to the fire, so I only work with people who are very serious about making changes in their businesses."

Maybe she didn't want new clients. Of course, she had no idea how hard I was willing to work. I waited to see how good she really was before pursuing the issue any further.

After introducing her to the attendees, I took a seat at the front table. Within the first three minutes of Reneé's keynote, I realized why she'd been so confident. Reneé was the real deal. She had us in the palm of her hand, taking us on an emotional rollercoaster—from belly laughs to tears—during her forty-minute talk. Reneé inspired me more than any speaker I'd ever heard. Not once did I look up at her and think, *I could totally do that.* My thoughts were more along the lines of: *I'm not anywhere near that funny. I don't have any stories to tell that would relate to people like she does. No wonder she'd made a business of making people laugh.*

After the event, she complimented, "You were an incredible emcee. Are you available for hire?"

I laughed at the thought. "No, this is actually the first time I've emceed an event like this."

"Well, you were the best I've seen," she said. "You have a gift for being in the moment with people."

There it was again, that word. *A gift.*

"Back at you. You were the best speaker I'd ever heard," I said, knowing in my heart it wasn't the last I'd see of Reneé Rongen.

The following Monday, I got a Facebook message from Reneé. It said:

*You were my gold for the weekend. You were the most authentic and polished speaker, with natural extemporaneous style. Let's visit this week maybe on Wednesday if you are serious. Let me know your thoughts. Remember, I'm the one who holds your feet to the fire when you are ready.*

I felt it deep down in my toes: this woman would provide the exact support I needed to get my business moving. I scheduled my first face-to-face visit a few weeks later with Real Deal Reneé!

## Parallel Lives

A week after the event, I knew I needed to talk to Mom about our misunderstanding. At least that's what *she* kept calling it—*our* misunderstanding. To my way of thinking, I had clearly asked her to help me and, when she failed to keep up her end of the deal, I felt betrayed. We sat at my kitchen counter.

"I just feel like you're asking me to take the full blame for this misunderstanding," Mom started. "I specifically asked you on Tuesday and you said you didn't need me."

"Okay, I understand that, but I wish you'd quit calling it a misunderstanding. I had no idea that you didn't have the specifics written on your calendar. Your comment about me 'thinking about it for months when other people don't' was hurtful to me. I felt like you just blew me off."

"Well, I tried to ask and you didn't say anything. And when Jeremiah stopped by the house to get Bryn's formula, I felt hurt by the way he spoke to me," she admitted. "If I'm always going to feel this much pressure when I'm asked to watch your kids, I'm not sure I want to watch them as much anymore."

My heart sank. "Mom, I need you. I depend on you. I can't run my business without your support. And there's no one else I'd rather have watching my kids. When they're with you, I don't even have to think about what might be happening. I know that they're having a good time because they love being with you, and I know they're being well taken care of. You are an unbelievable comfort to me."

Her face softened. "Maybe I just needed to hear that."

Really? She didn't know she was important? I wondered how long it had been since I'd last told her how much I appreciated her. I couldn't remember. I'd been a brat. A whiny, selfish brat, thinking only about myself.

"Maybe you did," I said. "Obviously, I've forgotten to tell you that you are the saving grace of my life here in Oakes, especially with my kids being so young. I can't imagine what my life would be like without you."

For Mom to admit she needed a sincere compliment had to be as difficult as asking for help. In our family, we didn't toot our own horns. Compliments were not something we fished for. My mom had said what was on her mind. How could I be upset with her for that?

If she and I were books on a shelf, she would be the locked diary, a trove of delicious secrets and stories. But only a reader with the key could open it. Her stories didn't belong to just anyone. On the other hand, I'd be the worn, well-read book with a broken spine, the book refusing to close all the way, popping back open as soon as you set it down. I had a tendency to give too much away. *I shared.*

I never thought of my mother as a role model because we were always so different. She was private, introverted, quiet. She was a nurturer, content to be on the farm, along with her gardening tools and nature. I wanted a big, bold, audacious life full of people and excitement. I always thought her life was too simple, too boring, too mundane. I didn't want her life. I was destined for something larger and, by my youthful standards, better.

I always believed I was more like my father in many ways: gregarious, a people-lover, a risk-taker, career-focused. Dad knew what he wanted and he went after it with dogged determination. He nearly drove himself into the ground for his passion, his lifelong love affair with farming.

Moving back to Oakes, and my ensuing struggle to regain my groove, revealed that I wasn't actually much like my father at all in this regard. "Follow your passion," the widely accepted advice that never fully left my mind, left me feeling like a failure. I wasn't sure there was one solitary thing to which I could devote my entire life.

Now on the cusp of the most honest conversation I'd ever had with my mom, it was clear: I was more like her. She couldn't afford to recklessly pursue just one thing; she had too many other roles to play. As Mom raised children, cared for aging parents, and eventually accepted her role of farmer's wife, she continued to challenge herself to grow. She acquired many talents and pursued many dreams throughout her life. Her passion was not singular; she simply allowed herself to follow her interests. I finally saw her for the woman she was—quiet, but fierce; private, but with a story that mattered; nurturing, but with dreams of her own; introverted, yet needing people.

Since moving back, I had watched my mother care for her loved ones in ways that I never believed I was capable of. I only hoped that, when called to, I could serve the people in my life as honestly and fully as she had. In spite of our significant differences, we chose to love each other, to live together. Good or bad, the things that happened in my life became real when I shared them with her. I was blessed to call my mother a friend, the kind of friend that transcends any category.

She was the first Nestie in my life.

For the first time, I could clearly see the parallels between our lives. I was as proud of this resemblance as the physical one we bear.

## Finding Focus

As we sat across from one another in a booth in a quaint little deli in Fargo, Reneé pushed me to get clear on my target audience. This had been my struggle from the beginning of my business. I had provided value in the business sector and was a mom living in a small town. Who could I best serve with my work?

Tailoring my message exclusively to moms wasn't working; my business hadn't set the world on fire. Deeply disappointed, I had had to cancel my second offering of the Busy Mom's Retreat because of lack of interest. I'd learned that, sadly, mothers rarely were willing to invest money in themselves. Moms made the world go around, spending time, money, and energy on their children, but ask them to devote time to self-improvement and they shuddered at the concept. I didn't want to compete with money set aside for pedicures, massages, drinks with friends, or any other legitimate way a mom might spend money on herself. I couldn't squeeze blood from a stone.

After drilling me with questions and listening closely to my answers, Reneé brightened. "I know who you should serve! But you're probably not going to like it much."

"By all means, tell me." Exhausted from re-hashing what felt like a long line of failures since I'd started my business, I needed someone to tell me what to do.

"People in rural America need you," she announced.

Really? Rural America? How could I get paid to speak to rural America? To be clear, being paid was no longer about great shoes; I needed to contribute to our household's bottom line. I was hungry to make an impact worthy of an income. I was ready for change.

"I know it's not sexy," Reneé admitted. "But think about it. You grew up there, you moved back there, you're supporting your hubby in a family-owned business, you now have kids there. If I asked you to write down everything you can about living in a small town and then put them into buckets labeled Sad, Endearing, Depressing, Frustrating, Amazing, do you think you could do it?"

"Of course, easily," I said, feeling the nip of excitement. "My whole life is speaking material, even the times I come to the big city of Fargo. I don't get how I'll make money at it, but the thought of focusing on my experience in Oakes makes me feel like I can give up trying to live two lives."

One life. That's what I had hoped for since moving home to Oakes. One life, filled with people I care about. I didn't want to compartmentalize my life into Work and Family. I wanted them intertwined. It would be messier and more chaotic, but richer.

I would focus on people in rural America. It was a new kind of homecoming.

## Step into the Ring

Living in a small town was a trade-off. You couldn't experience the quaintness of a Norman Rockwell portrait without the challenges that such intimacy created. To put it plainly, everyone was in your business. While stifling at times (like when I really did want to be left alone or go unnoticed in public), that intimacy is, in truth, what allowed us to take care of each other. Casseroles only got delivered when people knew what was going on.

Since becoming a mom, I worried that the intimacy of Oakes would keep my kids from living freely, that they'd be as plagued by the concern of what everyone else thought as I had been growing up.

One Saturday in late April, I hollered at the boys, "Come on, guys, we're going to the grocery store!"

"Mom, can I dress up like a superhero?" asked Carter, three-and-a-half.

"To go to the grocery store?"

"Yeah."

There were battles worth fighting, I figured, but this certainly wasn't one of them. "Sure. Why not?"

He ran downstairs and soon bounded back up, striking a pose with hands on his hips. Outfitted in a full Spiderman costume—

with muscles, a flashing spider on his chest, and a head mask, you couldn't tell he was Carter Undem.

I laughed. "Let's go get some produce, Spidey!"

"Really, Mom?" asked five-year-old Andrew, questioning my decision. "We can do that?" His doubt had a legitimate source: every time we left the house, we saw people we knew.

"Sure. Who says we can't?"

He dashed to the basement and returned wearing his Captain America mask and cape, wielding a sword and a shield.

I buckled Brynlee into her car seat while the superheroes jumped in the back. We cruised along the two-minute trip. When I paused at the town's solitary stoplight, I glanced in the rearview mirror. Andrew fidgeted and wore a worried expression. I pulled into the parking lot.

"Mom," he asked, "what if people laugh at me?"

I tried to be nonchalant. "Well, Andrew, what if they do?"

While I unsnapped Brynlee, Carter jumped out of the car in all his superhero glory. We watched as Andrew removed every piece of his costume. Maybe, as a firstborn child, he was stricken with the "disease to please." Maybe, he thought Carter looked cooler and wished he'd chosen a costume that made him as unrecognizable.

Whatever his reason, I decided he needed a strong example. Even when afraid of criticism, I vowed, I would step into the ring. I had some experience under my belt already by offering the Dale Carnegie Course in Oakes to my neighbors and community members. I had never been so intimately connected to participants in any program I'd ever before facilitated; it was like training a room full of extended family members. In this little town, I couldn't be anything other than what I preached. Everyone would know and see me as a fraud. That was why I had tried to fly under the radar for so long; if no one knew what my work was, they couldn't really judge me.

All those concerns had bubbled to the surface as I prepared for my first session with them.

Small towns needed sources of inspiration. To be challenged to grow. To be reminded that, even though it's scary, we could do different and unique things even with the threat of criticism. And the threat was imminent; we couldn't change other people who were hard-wired for opinions and gossip. Much better to give them something exciting to talk about!

It involved uncomfortable words: vulnerable, risky, scary. We would have to take off the masks because genuine connection could only happen when we let our guard down and people in.

If I wanted my children to live boldly and let go of what other people might be thinking about them, the only way to teach them was to show them. I was ready to be the role model that they needed me to be.

## Family Traditions

As I sat in my home office trying to finish my homework for my coaching call with Reneé, my cell phone buzzed on my desk. I glanced over and saw Jeremiah was calling. "Hey. What's up?"

"I'm having a completely shitty morning," said Jeremiah. "I'm broken down again and no one has the part we need, so it looks like I'll have time to eat a real lunch today. Any chance you can bring me something?"

"Sure. What do you want?"

"Just grab anything that sounds good."

I looked at my watch and realized I probably wasn't going to finish what I'd set out to do. Closing my laptop, I left the house and hopped in the car to get Jeremiah some lunch. Being a vastly different farmwife than Grandma Rodine, I often wondered if she'd be appalled that I nearly always purchased the food I took to the field. *She'd be so thrilled we're living here,* I decided, *she probably wouldn't care.*

After picking up a hamburger and fries special from the little diner that was formerly the Dairy Queen where Dad and Mom first met, I drove west on County Road 3 to meet Jeremiah at The Farm.

The Farm was the site that housed the commercial farming operation, formerly the homestead of Grandpa and Grandma Rodine.

The year prior, Dad had the farmhouse demolished and leveled the ground, making it impossible to tell how it used to appear.

As I opened the door to the hallway outside Jeremiah's office in the shop, I noticed the pictures lining the walls. The first, dated 1910, featured the homestead. The landscape consisted of one small barn, a tiny house, a one-room granary, and nearly no trees. Another captured Grandpa and Grandma Rodine standing next to their Allis-Chalmers tractor. One of the photos showed Dad driving down a gravel prairie trail in a tractor, his big, white-toothed grin flashing from the cab. Finally, there was an aerial shot of the present day commercial farm with its modern buildings.

Although I had certainly seen these pictures before, I marveled. From the humble beginnings of my great-great grandfather to the successful operation the farm had become today, we were connected to it all. The land, the buildings, the people, the legacy. Even though this choice to move back was at my urging, it would have never worked without Jeremiah's determination and willingness.

I greeted him and handed him his lunch as he sat down at the table. "I'm really proud of you. I haven't said that enough. But seriously, the fact that you're out here learning how to do this, with no prior background, deserves some praise. Thank you for what you do for our family. I'm sorry I haven't said it enough."

He looked at me with curiosity, as if my kind words were a precursor to the bad news that I'd totaled my car or something. I didn't hand out compliments easily. "Uh, thanks," he said. I squeezed his arm and let him eat in peace, knowing he'd had a tough morning with machinery breakdowns.

Although this impromptu trip to the farm hadn't been on my agenda for the day, I felt a deep satisfaction for having the opportunity to be there for Jeremiah when he needed me.

## Omitting the Ordinary

In May, Jonda's son, Jon, graduated from high school. At his graduation party, my cell phone rang.

"Can you come pick us up, honey?" Dad asked.

"Why do you need me to pick you up? Aren't you coming here to Jon's party?"

"Can't. We were in a car accident," he said.

"What! Are you both okay?"

Always the farmer, he answered, "Yeah, we're okay. But our car sure isn't."

I left my kids with Jonda and headed toward the farm. When I saw flashing police lights from the highway, I turned onto our gravel road and pulled to a stop at the railroad tracks. I gasped when I saw my parents' car. The front end was smashed in and the front tire had blown off.

I immediately hugged Mom, who was visibly shaken. We listened as Dad gave his statement to the police.

Always a cautious driver, when Dad saw a truck coming down the dusty gravel road, he pulled to the right side of the road to avoid getting a rock chip in his windshield. A car, speeding too fast for the gravel, appeared immediately behind the truck. The driver spun out of control and hurled toward my parents, giving my dad little time to react. Had Dad not already pulled so far over, they would have been hit head on.

I grabbed Dad and buried my face in his chest. "I don't hug you enough. This could have been really, really bad."

In an instant, my parents could have been snatched away. Did they know what they meant to me? Had I told them? Did I show them? Had I spent enough time with them? Did my kids know how wonderful my parents are?

At a recent Bible study, we were urged to create a list of one thousand gifts, numbering the simple blessings we receive each day. I had been writing down at least five every night before my head hit the pillow. The evening of the car accident, I realized I'd neglected my list for a month. Instead, I had focused on the busyness and the stress. I forgot about the blessings in my life. I lacked gratitude.

Even though I hadn't looked for them, I knew there were always, always, always things to acknowledge. I knew a daily reflection and accounting helped me see the world through a sharper lens.

After I took my parents to the farmhouse and got my kids home and to bed, I settled in a chair with my journal, reflecting. I looked back on the month and the day-to-day things I appreciated about it. I clicked my pen and started a growing list:

- drinking cool water with lemon
- taking Carter and Brynlee to the greenhouse to buy flowers
- planting shrubs with Andrew
- Andrew's perfect attendance in kindergarten, no sick days
- Dad driving cautiously
- smelling freshly mowed grass
- cows mooing in the pasture

- my gift of singing, sharing with the residents at the Manor
- the little ponytail on the top of Brynlee's head

Not a single gift was flashy or glamorous. In rural Oakes, life was simple and ordinary, offering up simple and ordinary gifts. The biggest gifts were in the small moments. I just needed to look for them.

## Mommy's Got a Brand New Groove

As promised, Reneé held my feet to the fire. She pushed hard and I rose to the challenge of building a business around my life in a small town.

It was as if Reneé had handed me a magic pair of glasses and said, "Here, put these on. Now, go home and look around a bit."

My little town looked different to me now.

Smiling, I left my house unlocked and garage doors opened wide, knowing this was totally normal. We felt safe enough to leave our homes open.

The sunrise was a sight to behold. Unlike big cities, there wasn't a building in town tall enough to hide our spectacular view of the wide expanse of sky.

As we strolled around Oakes—the boys on their bikes and Brynlee in her stroller, I was greeted by every person I met. I oftentimes completely stopped to visit and catch up. A historically fast walker, talker, and all-around *mover*, I had always been a little frustrated by the pace of rural living. Now, I found myself savoring the times when we didn't feel rushed and pushed.

Even in town we were surrounded by nature, serenaded by cows that went to pasture directly across the highway from our house.

Geese, glad to return to North Dakota after traveling for the winter, filled the sky with their coming home songs.

As we returned to our neighborhood, we saw the familiar faces of the kids who lived there as they rode their bikes and motorized John Deere toys right down the middle of the street. Our kids didn't really watch out for cars. The cars watched out for them.

I knew I'd never again struggle to answer the question, "What do you do for fun there?"

All the experiences I'd had in Oakes—and those yet to come—were stories to be told. From the funny to the frustrating, the hilarious to the heinous, I'd never run out of material and I'd never get bored in my work.

The whole time I'd been trying to get my groove back, I was searching for the woman I once was. I wanted to be professional Rebecca who was career-oriented, known for her ability to influence positive change in her workplace. I wanted to be the Rebecca who was successful. But I couldn't go back. I wasn't that woman anymore. I was no longer a woman solely defined by her value to the workplace.

As I reveled in my little town, I also reveled in the woman I'd become.

I was a different person than when I'd first found my groove in a banking role in Fargo. Children changed me. When Andrew was born, I wanted to be a working mom, emphasis on *working*. After having Carter and Brynlee, more of my heart embraced motherhood and I wanted to be a mommy that worked, emphasis on *mommy*. This change was unexpected and, initially unwelcomed. I had always pictured myself in a business suit, balancing my high-priced coffee and a cell phone—while pushing a stroller only when necessary.

Living in a small town changed me. Even as I secured jobs close to what I'd dreamed of, having an "important" career (that I didn't share with my community) never felt quite right.

Becoming a farmer's wife changed me. Jeremiah and I had become closer now than we'd ever been as I settled into those responsibilities and routines. I still struggled with bouts of resentment, especially during the busy seasons, but it was undeniable how much he loved farming. And I loved his commitment to providing for our family.

In short, *life* changed me.

As it turned out, the dream I was pursuing didn't fit me anymore. I needed to redefine what success meant for me. Being a goal-oriented person, I had always believed success was simply a matter of achievement. Set a goal, develop a plan, execute your plan, and achieve your goal. Bam. Success. Success was measurable, objective, and evident to other people. The process should yield a relatively straight line. A clear path from Point A to Point B.

As I looked back on my journey, the path was anything but a straight line. In fact, the line was so zigged and zagged, you'd swear it was navigated by a drunkard or a flighty individual with no direction or life goals.

My children took me down unexplored paths, Jeremiah's needs had me venturing off, each job I accepted and eventually left had me weaving and bobbing all over the place, all of which eventually caused me to look up and ask, "Wait. Where was I going?"

Here's what I realized: I *liked* my journey.

None of those detours were mistakes. None of those detours were steps in the wrong direction. None of those choices made me a failure.

Success was no longer about status, what other people thought about my choices, or who might be pleased or displeased along the way. I had created my own definition, a definition that allowed for wandering. I liked the unexpected blessings that arose when I allowed myself to simply enjoy the journey.

Success now could be a quick trip to deliver a store-bought lunch to the field for my hubby. It could be me watching in silent understanding as my kids struggle with a craft project. It could be nothing more than sharing a cup of coffee with Mom.

And that felt pretty darn groovy.

With Reneé's help, I created my first keynote later that summer and delivered it to a group of fifty women. Mom and Noreen sat near the front and several other women from Oakes attended. Prior to this, I had never delivered a one-hour keynote without notes and a Power Point. This time, I offered only the simplicity of my stories about small-town life. Although nervous, I felt more alive on that stage in a little North Dakota town than anything I'd done in the corporate scene. When I was in high school, Mom intuitively believed I could have a career as a motivational speaker. Just as she'd been so many times before, Mom was right.

It was a full circle moment for me.

All of my life roles meshed. In my message, I spoke about being a daughter, a mother, a business owner, and a farmer's wife. There was no part of my life that I had to omit. All of my *gifts* meshed. I could be dramatic, funny, extemporaneous, and witty all while delivering real value to people in their own small town. I could focus on the only thing that I ever would have considered my *passion*: people.

The two conditions that afflicted me most of my life were in remission: the disease to please and perfectionism. I no longer pursued the smart decision; I fully embraced that truth that I learn from doing. It wasn't about perfect planning; it was about learning as I go.

When Mom called the next day to see how I felt about my talk, I asked for her honest feedback. "Honey, I'm so proud of you," she said in a wavering voice. "You were wonderful."

To date, that keynote was my best work.

It was clear.

Mommy had gotten her groove back.

# Home

Later that summer, I was asked to offer a training session for a Dale Carnegie client in Minneapolis. The timing worked out perfectly with the event on the Thursday afternoon of a weekend our little family had already planned there. A group of Jeremiah's high school friends and their families were attending a Twins game at Target Field. I had never been and this was our sons' first Big League experience.

We reiterated to the boys the importance of watching for traffic and staying close to Dad and Mom, our customary cautions when traveling to a city. And, hilariously, admitted that, no, we don't in fact "know everyone here."

On the second day, we found ourselves traveling back to our hotel during rush hour; our boys had never seen anything like it. We were in the middle of a four-lane highway, surrounded by cars. We weren't moving. At all.

Andrew demanded, "Dad! Why don't you go?"

"Why are we just sitting here?" Carter echoed.

"I hate the city," Jeremiah grumbled. "This just sucks." His more, er, vibrant adjectives were hard to catch because he was conscientious enough to keep his voice low with little ears in the car.

I chuckled to myself. After explaining to the boys that we have to be patient (and starting another movie for them to watch as a distraction), I was struck with a new realization. This was the first trip I'd taken to a city, since moving back to Oakes, when I truly didn't have a single ounce of yearning to live there. I had made most of my trips to bigger cities for work. Alone. The exhilaration and excitement didn't feel the same with my kids along. Knowing I'd soon return to the quiet, slower pace, and, Lord help me, the mundane, made the trip even more enjoyable. I was anxious to return to our very own Mayberry.

I looked at my frazzled husband. "Do you wish we were on County Road 3 heading west out of Oakes to The Farm?"

"Absolutely. This traffic is nuts!"

I shared my thoughts and yearnings. In his deadpan, no bullshit way, he simply said, "Well, good. It's about time you came around, because I have no desire to live here, whatsoever."

As we pulled into Oakes at the close of our weekend, Andrew yelled from the backseat, "Yay! We're home!"

I smiled with a deep satisfaction at the significance of the word. We certainly were.

# Repurposed

One of the things my mom and I have always enjoyed is the process of repurposing a piece of furniture. We love the idea of taking something old and giving it new life. There's something almost romantic about the process. The key to repurposing furniture is to look beyond the item's current state to imagine what it could be. The process requires vision. We can't be deterred by ugly fabric or chipped paint.

Also, there must be a love or admiration for the original piece. Sometimes, the piece just "speaks" to us. Maybe the "bones" of a dresser are in good condition, maybe the clean lines of a chair grab our attention, or the intricate detailing of the arm on a sofa appeals to our taste. There has to be something about it that makes us want to bring it home and give it a facelift.

Repurposing furniture can be a lot of work. For wood pieces such as dressers, tables, and armoires, we might repair hinges and legs. A fresh coat of paint often makes even the most outdated furniture beautiful again. Painting is typically more involved than just slapping on a fresh coat of paint. Projects often include sanding, priming, more sanding, painting, and more sanding. It's amazing how a little sanding and painting can reveal a diamond in the rough.

Depending on the project, replacing hardware, applying antique finishes, or stenciling on the piece might be in order as well. Then, there's the chance it won't turn out like we'd hoped. Sometimes we need to tweak the finish or the paint color to get the desired effect.

Repurposing furniture is not everyone's thing; some people prefer buying their furniture shiny and new. No judgment; that doesn't make them somehow worse. It's just not a process everyone is willing to embark upon.

Returning to Oakes and making a new life here has been a similar process. I treasure the memories of my upbringing in rural North Dakota. If I hadn't enjoyed it at all, the work required to restore it would never be worthwhile. I loved my youth and the people from my youth enough to come back and build something new on that foundation.

But it's crucial to realize that I couldn't leave the piece just as it was. If Oakes was meant to be my future, I'd have to give it new life or I would feel like I was staring at an old wardrobe that had outlived its usefulness. I needed to make Oakes feel like it was mine. Not my parents'. Not my grandparents'. Not high school Becky's. Not Tom and Jean Rodine's daughter's. Not even Jeremiah Undem's wife's. I needed to figure out how to make it Rebecca's.

Like applying an antiquing technique, each new memory and experience I create here changes the way Oakes looks. As people I love die and as my babies were born, I see less and less of the original piece. But I can't forget entirely what it once was. And I don't want to. Oakes is both old and new at the same time.

I can't say for sure that this piece of furniture will always have a place in my home. No one knows what tomorrow will bring. But as long as I'm here, I will embrace the simplicity of rural living, I will enjoy the journey—including the occasional wandering, and I will be grateful for the presence of My People—the village, my parents, and my own little family.

Like Grandma Dorothy always said, "Family is everything."

# Epilogue

When I first set out to write my book, this book wasn't it. I originally submitted a manuscript more on par with my blog articles, offering advice and helpful suggestions to people who were on a journey to get their grooves back.

When my editor, the incomparable Carol McAdoo Rehme, first pushed, er, gently nudged, me to write this book as a memoir, I was blindsided with feelings of unworthiness. I thought, *What? You want me to write my story? Who on earth is going to care about my story? My story isn't special. My story doesn't matter.*

You probably picked up that I'm a bit of a control freak with a little OCD—crowned with a pile of enormous emotions. In short, I'm my own shade of crazy. (I know … you want to hang out with me, don't you?) I continually find ways to get in my own way. I can talk myself out of just about anything, and I like to use the guise of my choices being "smart" to justify my decisions.

The fear and the uncertainty that swirled around writing and publishing this book was like nothing I'd ever experienced before. I was so afraid that people wouldn't care or, worse yet, they'd make fun of what I'd created. My story would be a joke to people.

I told myself that my original book was safer, easier to write, and maybe a smarter choice. After all, people like the "how" of a process and might be upset that this book doesn't include all of my hard-hitting wisdom. (Read that in sarcasm font.)

Even though that all might be true, I knew I needed to challenge myself to do the hard work. I have no desire to reach the end of my life, whenever that may be, and say, "Well, that was safe and easy."

I want to make a lasting impact. I want to live my life to the fullest. I want to be a role model for my children. The path to accomplish those things is not likely to be safe or easy.

There are two things I know for sure. (And no, I'm not trying to rival Oprah here.) The first is that I'm really not in control of much. Life will throw me curveballs and, sometimes, bad things will happen. None of what happens to me is within my control. My plan will always be trumped by *The Plan*.

The second is that I'm a constantly evolving person. As I change and grow, my perspective on life shifts. How I feel about something today may differ immensely from how I'll feel about that same thing five years from now. There is absolutely no way to know how I'm going to feel about something until I'm standing right in front of it.

Those two truths allowed me to relax into the uncertainty of the unknown. To embrace the struggle of not having all the answers and moving forward anyway.

To enjoy the journey—wandering included.

As I spent countless hours interviewing my mom and dad and talking to Jeremiah and writing and rewriting this story, I made a discovery: My story matters. Everyone has a story. Everyone's story matters.

This process of getting your groove back is a journey. And, for me, it doesn't end here. It doesn't have to end here for you either. *Your* story matters and I would love to hear it.

Be on the lookout for *How Mommy Got Her Groove Back*[TM]— *The Groovefinder's Guide Series*. I'll be sharing hard-hitting wisdom, the lessons I learned, and practical advice you can apply to your own groove journey.

Whether we continue the journey together or separately, I hope you find the courage to embrace your detours. Each one offers a new path to explore and there's always something to be learned. Here's to finding *your* groove!